SpringerBriefs in Education

Open and Distance Education

Series editors

Insung Jung, International Christian University, Mitaka, Tokyo, Japan
Olaf Zawacki-Richter, University of Oldenburg, Oldenburg, Niedersachsen, Germany

More information about this series at http://www.springer.com/series/15238

Olaf Zawacki-Richter · Adnan Qayyum
Editors

Open and Distance Education in Asia, Africa and the Middle East

National Perspectives in a Digital Age

 Springer Open

Editors
Olaf Zawacki-Richter
Institute of Education
University of Oldenburg
Oldenburg, Niedersachsen, Germany

Adnan Qayyum
Pennsylvania State University
State College, PA, USA

ISSN 2211-1921   ISSN 2211-193X   (electronic)
SpringerBriefs in Education
ISSN 2509-4335   ISSN 2509-4343   (electronic)
SpringerBriefs in Open and Distance Education
ISBN 978-981-13-5786-2   ISBN 978-981-13-5787-9   (eBook)
https://doi.org/10.1007/978-981-13-5787-9

Library of Congress Control Number: 2018966401

This Springer imprint is published by the registered company Springer Nature Singapore Pte Ltd.
The registered company address is: 152 Beach Road, #21-01/04 Gateway East, Singapore 189721, Singapore

This book is dedicated to the memory of Colin Latchem. Colin contributed the Australia chapter in the first volume of these books. He was an important advocate of non-formal, open and distance education. His thoughtful contributions to the field will be missed.

Contents

Chapter 1
Introduction

Olaf Zawacki-Richter and Adnan Qayyum

Introduction

Since the mid 1990s, the digital transformation has changed the face of open and distance education as we had known it. Already in 1999, Alan Tait observed that "the secret garden of open and distance learning has become public, and many institutions are moving from single conventional mode activity to dual mode activity" (p. 141) and Kearsley (1998) even claimed that "distance education has become mainstream" (p. 1). Indeed, during the last 20 years distance education has moved from the fringes into the center of mainstream education provision (see Xiao, 2018, for a recent analysis). This is specially the case in the higher education sector where today in some countries—supported by enormous state funding programs like in Germany—almost all higher education institutions are offering some sort of online education, ranging from web-enhanced face to face teaching practices to fully online programs on an international scale—although they often do not label this distance education and use terms such as online, flexible or blended learning.

The process of the digital transformation—the "digital turn" (Westera, 2013)—affects all segments of society and economic sectors. Different nations and educational systems are responding differently to the macro process of digitalization. Some national systems are more advanced and ahead on the road by making the digitalization of teaching and learning a strategic goal for development and innovation already over a decade ago (e.g. South Korea) while in other countries distance education was recognized as a validated and accredited form of education provision only

O. Zawacki-Richter (✉)
Carl von Ossietzky University of Oldenburg, Oldenburg, Germany
e-mail: olaf.zawacki.richter@uni-oldenburg.de

A. Qayyum
Pennsylvania State University, State College, USA
e-mail: adnan@psu.edu

© The Author(s) 2019   1
O. Zawacki-Richter and A. Qayyum (eds.), *Open and Distance Education in Asia,*
Africa and the Middle East, SpringerBriefs in Open and Distance Education,
https://doi.org/10.1007/978-981-13-5787-9_1

in the recent past, now witnessing enormous growth rates of enrollments in online distance education with private institutions massively stepping into this market (e.g. Brazil).

The transformation of teaching and learning in a digital age presents a dramatic challenge of innovation and change for the majority of 'conventional' universities. Higher education institutions throughout the world have undergone changes to innovate teaching and learning processes by implementing infrastructures for educational technology and developing organizational support structures for students and faculty.

Distance teaching institutions have always been spearheading the application of new and emerging media, because in distance education media have always been used to bridge the gap students and the teaching institutions and among learners. Starting in the mid 1990s, the Internet and new information and communication technologies paved the way for overcoming the notion of distance education as an isolated form of learning. However, also traditional distance teaching universities are still struggling to make the transition from correspondence to online distance education (e.g. in South Africa).

In order to avoid that we reinvent the wheel in this very dynamic process of digital transformation, it is important that we learn from past experiences of open and distance education systems, covering over a century of theory, research and practice in the field (e.g. in the UK, Germany, South Africa and Russia).

The present book is the second volume in which we set out to explore, compare and contrast open and distance education systems in various countries. The first volume "Open and Distance Education in Australia, Europe and the Americas" covered national systems in Australia, Brazil, Canada, Germany, the UK and the USA. The goal is to describe different approaches and models of the relationship between distance education and higher education in each country by addressing the following questions:

1. What is the function and position of distance education within the national higher education system?
2. Which are the major DE teaching and research institutions?
3. What is the history and past of distance education including online education?
4. What is the relationship between DE and more established and older campus-based, residential institutions?
5. What is the relationship between public and private sector online and distance education?
6. What are the regulatory frameworks for DE? What are important policies for online and distance education?
7. What are estimated student enrollments for online and distance education programs?
8. What are probably important future developments and issues for online and distance education?

Structure of the Book

The countries are presented in alphabetical order. Each chapter is complemented by commentary written by an expert from each country. The aim of the commentaries is not to critique the chapters but to offer another perspective on each system and to highlight and emphasize certain aspects that are important from the experts' point of view.

Chapter 2 is about China. Wei Li and Na Chen from the Department of Comparative Education at the Open University of China emphasize the importance of online and open learning to provide services for lifelong learning for all. The Open University of China is the biggest university of the world in terms of student enrollments. It is a network with a headquarter in Beijing and 44 branches and about 3,000 study centers throughout the country. A path-breaking initiative towards lifelong learning is the creation of the "Credit Bank" for the accreditation, accumulation and transfer of formal and informal learning outcomes. An "Online Credit Bank Platform" was launched in November 2017 to support the accreditation and recognition of prior learning. The share of online enrollments in higher education reached 17% (6.45 Million students) in 2016. However, there is much room for potential growth of ODE in China. There are more than 2,900 higher education institutions in the country, but up to now only 67 campus-based universities and the Open University Network offer online degree programs.

It is interesting to note that the beginnings of Indian distance education were influenced by the Russian system. A delegation of the University Grants Commission visited the Soviet Union in 1961 to study their system of correspondence education and evening classes. Higher education expanded tremendously after independence in 1947. Today, the higher education system in India is a giant, with over 29 Million students, 712 universities and over 36,000 colleges—and this is still not enough too meet the huge demand for tertiary education of India's growing population. The authors, Santosh Panda and Suresh Garg, are from the Indira Gandhi National Open University (IGNOU), which is the central state university (founded in 1985) that coordinates distance education systems and programs throughout the country.

A team of authors from Russia and Germany, Olaf Zawacki-Richter, Sergey Kulikov, Diana Püplichhuysen, and Daria Khanolainen, describe the changes that have occurred in distance education in Russia and the former Soviet Union. There is a long tradition of distance education in Russia starting after the October Revolution in the second decade of the 20th century. Today, about 50% of all students in Russia are enrolled in distance education programs with a peak in 2009/2010. However, Russia is facing a dramatic "demographic hole": According to official statistics, the number of 15–19-year olds fell by one third from 2009 to 2014. In the same time period, the number of distance education students decreased from 4.1 to 2.6 million students. The Russian higher education system has undergone substantial reforms in recent years, investing in "elite" higher education institutions and "modern" distance education (i.e. e-learning, MOOCs, OERs) to overcome quality problems in print-based distance education and to reach international target groups.

Paul Prinsloo writes about South Africa, which is the country where the first dedicated distance teaching university was established in 1873. After 2004 and until 2014 the University of South Africa (UNISA) was the only public distance teaching university in South Africa. Nelson Mandela was a student at UNISA during his time of imprisonment on Robben Island. UNISA is a "big ship" with over 400,000 students. As Kok, Bester and Esterhuizen (2018) write in their current article "Late departures from paper-based to supported networked learning in South Africa", the transition from correspondence education to online learning represents a great challenge, especially in a developing country where reliable power supply and access to the Internet at affordable costs cannot be taken for granted in rural as well as metropolitan areas. The implications of introducing interactive online learning are discussed. In this context, it is important to find the right balance between the introduction of personalized and tutor-led online seminars and the provision of self-study materials for independent distance learning while maintaining economies of scale to provide affordable higher education opportunities for all.

Cheolil Lim, Jihyunb Lee and Hyosun Choi report on a process of radical innovation and enormous growth of online education in South Korea. They describe this development starting with the foundation of the Korea National Open University in 1972. Distance education became widely used, but with the emergence of the Internet between 1995 and 2009 a period of rapid growth gained momentum with strong support and funding from the Ministry of Education in South Korea. In 1997 the Korea Multimedia Education Center was established to facilitate education innovation at traditional campus-based universities and to support the establishment of so called "cyberuniversities" of which 21 exist today. Supporting lifelong learning was given a top priority by the Korean government, and online distance education has played a prominent role in providing learning opportunities throughout the lifespan. It is remarkable that 79% of high school graduates in South Korea enter a higher education institution. Despite this extraordinary progress in terms of digitalization of teaching and learning and access to higher education, some challenges remain. We are reminded by Insung Jung that there is still much potential for widening access for disadvantaged groups in South Korea who do not reside in Soul or the larger metropolitan areas.

Yasar Kondakci, Svenja Bedenlier and Cengiz Hakan Aydin provide an insightful overview of the open and distance education system in Turkey, where Anadolu University (established in 1982) in Eskisehir is one of the "mega-universities" with over one million active distance education students. Also in Turkey, the residential higher education system has been expanding immensely. In the late 1970s and 80s higher education was a privilege of a few. The 27 conventional universities provided only places for less than 6% of an age cohort. The number of universities increased from 27 in 1982 to 184 public and private universities in 2017. Open and distance education, particularly Anadolu University's ODL system, has been playing a major role in Turkish Higher Education by providing equal education opportunity to millions since 1982. Based on the latest figures of the Higher Education Council of Turkey (2016–2017 academic year) of the total number of ODL students in Turkey, around 1.2 million of them are actively pursuing their studies in different programs of Anadolu University. The quality assurance of these programs is critical for the reputation and status of online, open and distance education, in order to convince employers that degrees earned at a distance are at least as good as degrees from traditional campus-based institutions. In this context, it is notable, that since 2016 students who seek admission to Open Education programs and do not already hold a higher education degree or do not already study at another university have to take the same entrance examination as students who want to register in conventional undergraduate programs. So in fact, there is a recent development in Turkey, which reduces the openness of open education.

References

Kearsley, G. (1998). Distance education goes mainstream. *T. H. E. Journal*, *25*(10). Retrieved from https://thejournal.com/articles/1998/05/01/Distance-Education-Goes-Mainstream.aspx.

Kok, I., Bester, P., & Esterhuizen, H. (2018). Late departures from paper-based to supported networked learning in South Africa: Lessons learned. *International Journal of Distance Education Technologies, 16*(1), 56–75. https://doi.org/10.4018/IJDET.2018010104.

Tait, A. (1999). The convergence of distance and conventional education. In R. Mills & A. Tait (Eds.), *The convergence of distance and conventional education: Patterns of flexibility for the individual learner* (pp. 141–148). London: Routledge.

Westera, W. (2013). *The digital turn: How the internet transforms our existence*. Bloomington: AuthorHouse.

Xiao, J. (2018) On the margins or at the center? Distance education in higher education. *Distance Education, 39*(2), 259–274.

Chapter 2
China

Wei Li and Na Chen

Introduction

For the last four decades, distance higher education has played a very important role in China for knowledge and human resource development. This chapter presents a holistic view on the development of distance higher education in China with focus on the 21st century online higher education.

Distance education has always been an important part of the Chinese higher education system. Although the objectives vary somewhat from one time period to another, the main function of distance higher education is to provide Chinese people with access to knowledge. The present Chinese government regards current online higher education as an important way to promote lifelong learning and build a learning society. The *National Education Plan* (MOE, 2010) states that developing online higher education and ICT can meet the diversified and personalized learning demands of the public and contribute to the construction of an open and flexible lifelong education system. The student group of online higher education is diversified, including college-age youths, farmers, workers, the elderly, the disabled and the ethnic minority groups.

Brief History of Distance Higher Education

The history of distance higher education in China can be traced back to the late 1940s. It can be divided into three phases, according to the main types of transmission technology. The first phase (before 1979) is correspondence education, through the medium of postal communication; the second phase (between 1979 and 1998) is

W. Li (✉) · N. Chen
The Open University of China, No. 75, Fuxing Road, Haidian District, Beijing 100039, China
e-mail: liwei@ouchn.edu.cn

© The Author(s) 2019

O. Zawacki-Richter and A. Qayyum (eds.), *Open and Distance Education in Asia, Africa and the Middle East*, SpringerBriefs in Open and Distance Education, https://doi.org/10.1007/978-981-13-5787-9_2

radio and television education, making use of video and audio recordings, radio and television; the third phase (from 1999 until the present) is online education, using the Internet as the main medium of teaching and learning.

In 1999, the Ministry of Education (MOE) launched a pilot project entitling four campus-based universities (Tsinghua University, Zhejiang University, Beijing University of Posts and Telecommunications, and Hunan University), which had shown progress in the use of information and communication technologies (ICTs) in education, as well as the Central Radio and TV University (CRTVU)—now known as the Open University of China (OUC)—to offer diploma/degree programs in the so-called 'modern' distance education mode. This can be regarded as the beginning of online higher education in China.

Between 1999 and 2003, the MOE approved 68 universities to participate in the pilot project for online higher education. The CRTVU was the only Chinese university fully dedicated to online higher education. Among the selected campus-based universities, most were in Project 211, which is a project initiated in 1995 by MOE with the intent of constructing 100 national key universities and raising their research standards.

Since 1999, the above mentioned 68 universities have been the main providers of online higher education in China. As a result of their relentless efforts, China's distance higher education sector has entered into an era of burgeoning development. Distance higher education has made major contributions to the transformation of higher education from an elite system to a popular system. For example, the CRTVU, founded in 1979, is the largest and most influential distance higher education institution in China. According to an investigation conducted by the Strategic Office of the CRTVU (2010), from 1979 to 2009, it had a total of 7.2 million graduates, representing 24% of the total number of higher education graduates over the same period.

Scale and Funding of Distance Higher Education

Scale

The scale of distance higher education has increased year-by-year in China. As of 2017, there are over 2,900 higher education institutions, and the number of enrolled students has been on the rise, particularly in the past decade, with the rapid popularization of the Internet and growing demand for continuing education.

Online work, online learning and online life have become an indispensable part of life for the Chinese people for the last few years. President Xi (2014) remarks that China should aim to be not only a big Internet country, but an Internet powerhouse. China Internet Network Information Center (2017) reveals that from 2000 to 2017, the Internet penetration rate in China surged from 1.7% to 54.3%, and the number of Internet users increased from 22.5 million to 750 million. It is more than half

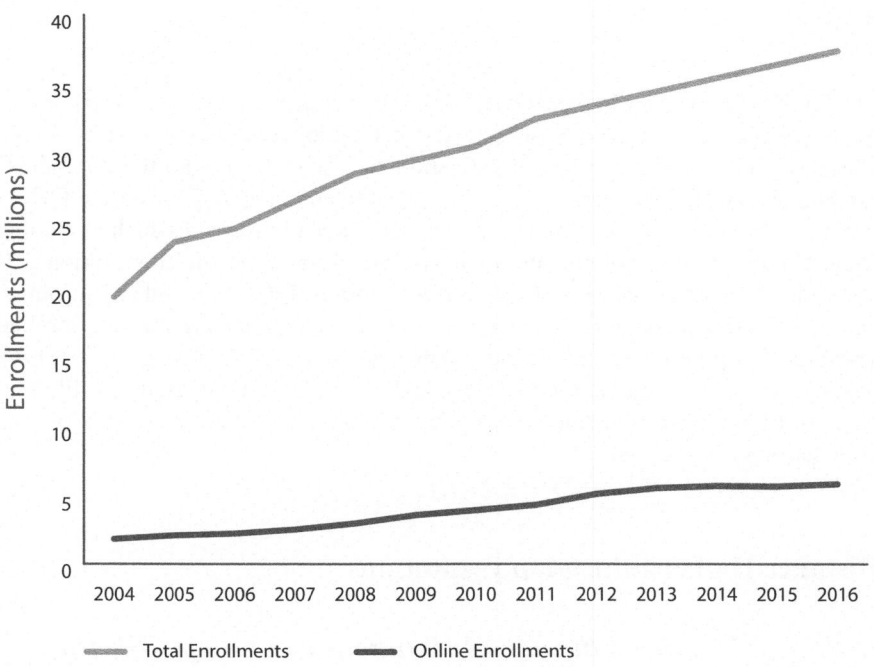

Fig. 2.1 Enrollment of online higher education in higher education system between 2004 and 2016 (million). *Source* Ministry of Education Website (http://www.moe.edu.cn/s78/A03/moe_560/jytjsj_ 2016/)

of the total Chinese population and constitutes the biggest group of Internet users around the world. And it provides a good basis for extending and facilitating online education.

There is an ongoing need for education in China. Li, Yao, and Chen (2014) point out that since 2004, China has become an ageing society and the ageing population will increase rapidly in the next 20 years. And with the improvement of security, medical insurance and pension services for the elderly, their demand for leisure education will grow and cannot be satisfied by campus-based universities. At the same time, the urbanization is accelerating, which raises the integration problems of farmers' work and life in urban areas. The National Bureau of Statistics (2015) shows that the percentage of the total population living in urban areas in China increased from 36.2% in 2000 to 56.1% in 2015. This urbanization process requires significant provision of continuing vocational training for farmers, in order to enhance their livelihood opportunities.

According to the statistics issued by the MOE (2016), the enrollment of online higher education in China has increased from 2.37 million to 6.45 million between 2004 and 2016, as it is shown in Fig. 2.1. And the share of the student number in the entire higher education system has risen from 11.9% to 17.4%.

Funding

The funding for distance higher education in China comes from two main sources—government grants and revenues such as students' tuition fees, charges for non-degree education and training, etc. An investigation by Yang (2014) into the 2012 OUC funding shows that, students' tuition fees constituted about 70% of all the OUC's revenues, and regarding the funding for the local open universities such as Beijing Open University, the government grants accounted for 30%, students' tuition fees 40% and other revenues 30%. It should be mentioned that the students in online degree education do not receive the government allocation like the students enrolled in offline full-time degree education. Many scholars, such as Zheng (2014), have conducted research into the funding issue and appealed for equal rights of different types of higher education students to grants from the government, but so far, this issue has not been resolved.

Distance Higher Education Institutions

Dedicated Distance Education Institutions and Campus-Based Institutions

The online education enrollment in these two systems—open universities and campus-based universities-differs. Figure 2.2 shows the changes of enrollment in these two systems between 2004 and 2015.

China's MOE (1999) states that the main factors that enabled the first four campus-based universities to offer online courses are that they enjoyed high educational standards and quality, had a good academic reputation, a well-defined operating plan, corresponding organizational infrastructure, staff, essential facilities and funds. At the beginning, Tsinghua University was the only one allowed to enroll online students nationwide. Beijing University of Posts and Telecommunications was only allowed to enroll students studying online in the posts and telecommunications sector, while Hunan University and Zhejiang University were only supposed to offer online courses within the provinces in which they were located. But soon, these universities were all allowed to enroll online students nationwide with the permission of MOE.

The online student number of the campus-based universities differs. The MOE (2015a) reports that, in 2014, Dalian University of Technology, Chongqing University, Beihang University, Jilin University and Central South University were the top five in terms of online student number, each with over 30,000 students studying online in degree programs.

It should be mentioned that the open universities and the campus-based institutions mainly provide certificates and academic degrees (associate, bachelor). And some campus-based universities offer online master degree programs with the approval of MOE.

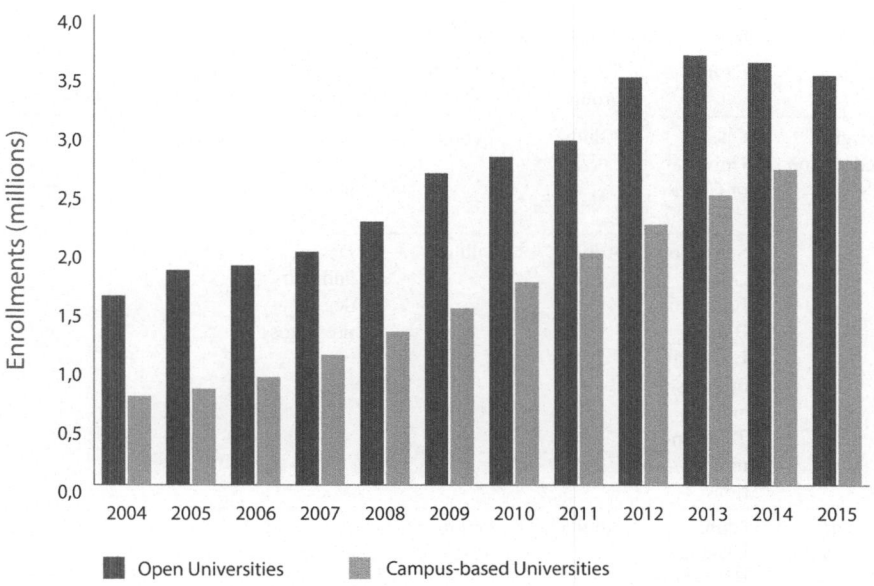

Fig. 2.2 Online education enrollment of Open Universities and the Campus-based Universities, between 2004 and 2015 (million). *Source* Ministry of Education (http://www.moe.edu.cn/jyb_sjzl/)

Public and Private Providers

At present, there are a considerable number and variety of distance education institutions in China (see Table 2.1), some of which are public and some are private. They can be classified by education level and target group.

The open universities and the campus-based universities play an important role in the public distance education sector, offering both degree and non-degree programs.

The private distance education sector, which includes private universities, Internet companies and corporate online institutions named as e-universities, usually provide non-degree programs. They offer mainly vocational and skills training, with more market-oriented courses. Their students have the prospect of gaining industry qualifications or skills certificates.

Regulatory Frameworks and Policies of Distance Higher Education

In China, there is no special legislation on distance higher education, but some education laws relate to distance education. For example, a distance higher education institution is required to comply with relevant provisions in the *Higher Education*

Table 2.1 Distance education institutions in China

Level	Example	Target group	Ownership	Scope of service	Date of launch	Gone public?
Higher education	Open University of China	Adults	Public	Degree and non-degree programs	1979	–
	School of Online Education, Beijing University of Posts and Telecommunications	Adults	Public	Degree and non-degree programs	1956	–
Adult education	China Distance Education Holdings Ltd.	Adults	Private	Professional certificates	2000	Yes
Various types and levels of education	Koolearn	All groups	Private	Foreign language training	2000	Yes
	Alibaba	All groups	Private	Early childhood education, professional training, etc.	2013	Yes

Law (1998). Li (2007) conducted research into regulations regarding the development of distance education in China, including access, price regulation, quality and information regulation, for which different administrative bodies are responsible. For example, access regulation rests mostly with national or local educational authorities, and price regulation is controlled by local price control authorities.

The central government formulates and releases policies on the regulation of distance higher education, and local governments make suggestions for implementation and put them into operation. The policies focus on different levels of targets. Some policy documents target the overall development of distance education, such as *Opinions on Developing China's Modern Distance Education* (1998) and *Provisional Regulations of Correspondence Education for Conventional Higher Education Institutions* (1987). Other policies target the organization and operation of distance education institutions, such as *Provisional Regulations for Radio & TV Universities* (1988) and *Opinions of the MOE on Ensuring Successful Operation of the Open*

University (2016). There are also documents dealing with practical distance higher education programs, such as *Notice of Research Program on Central Radio & TV University's Reform of Professional Training Mode and Pilot Projects in Open Education* (1999).

Several iconic events shaped the development of policies on distance higher education. Firstly, the *Notice on Comprehensive Universities Providing Correspondence Education* was issued in 1956, which marked the beginning of colleges delivering distance higher education through correspondence and evening courses. Secondly, the *Instruction Requesting Report of the MOE and Central Broadcasting Affairs Bureau on Establishing TV Universities* (issued in 1978) marked a new attempt to develop distance higher education via 'Radio & TV' universities. Thirdly, the release of the *Document on Initiating Pilot Programs for Modern Distance Education* in 1999 heralded the onset of online higher education, with participating universities expanded to both Radio & TV universities and campus-based universities. Fourthly, in 2010, the General Office of the State Council released the *Notice on Pilot Reform of the National Education System*, which mentioned the establishment of Open Universities based on Radio & TV universities.

Through years of efforts, China has gradually built up the regulatory framework for distance higher education and implemented policies to guide its development. However, there is still room for improvement in legislation and policy development. For example, there is a need for more formulation of legislation on online higher education, policy planning to guide the development of online higher education, and regulations and guidance on the setup of different types of online higher education institutions and their operation. Although the educational administration department has realized the urgency of further policy formulation and implementation, the process remains slow and needs to be accelerated.

Quality Assurance of Distance Higher Education

Quality assurance is a prominent issue in the development of distance higher education in China, high on the agendas of both the government and institutions. Distance higher education institutions, both public and private, are encouraged to build internal and external quality assurance systems.

To build an internal quality assurance system, distance higher education institutions normally create a set of quality standards, set up a special division with professional staff, develop quality-related strategies and policies, establish procedures and requirements, and conduct institutional quality self-evaluation. For example, Zhejiang University is one of the top universities in China and the first of the four campus-based universities to establish an online college. It formulated quality standards and set up a Quality Assurance Committee as well as a Center for Quality Control and Evaluation. It established a team of full-time professionals, issued guidelines for monitoring teaching quality, and carried out teaching inspection and supervision activities.

All the distance higher education institutions receive external quality evaluation and accreditation. External evaluators include national or local educational authorities, international organizations or industry associations. For example, educational authorities monitor and review quality assurance of distance higher education institutions. In 2001, the MOE initiated a quality review of the CRTVU and 22 local RTVUs. According to the MOE (2002) review report, all the institutions passed the review, with the exception of one local RTVU which was suspended, but passed a second review after one year of reforms. Between 2004 and 2007, the MOE carried out a holistic quality review of RTVUs. The evaluation activities were many and varied, including debriefings, reading materials, examining facilities, reviewing classes, holding a variety of symposiums, inspecting learning centers and so on. According to the MOE (2007a) review report, the CRTVU and 44 local RTVUs all passed the evaluation. At the same time, the MOE (2007b) launched a quality review of the campus-based universities, which all passed the evaluation as well.

Since 2004, it has been compulsory for distance higher education universities to submit annual quality reports to the MOE and undergo annual inspections, which is a government mandate for quality accreditation. Furthermore, there is a voluntary quality review of distance education institutions conducted by the associations, like International Council for Open and Distance Education (ICDE) and International Standardization Organization (ISO). In 2008, Shanghai RTVU applied for and passed the ICDE Quality Review. And in the same year, the Online College of East China University of Science and Technology applied for and acquired ISO 9001: 2000 QMS certification.

However, problems remain with both internal quality assurance and external quality supervision and evaluation. In terms of the former, there is room for improvement in the universities' quality assurance ability. It should be noted that although distance higher education institutions claim that they are devoted to building internal quality assurance, many of them still do not prioritize such activities. For example, in the evaluation report of the CRTVU, MOE (2007a) points out that the reform of teaching modes, particularly practical teaching, needed to be reinforced, and the professional development of the teaching staff should be strengthened. As the then-President of Shanghai RTVU Xu (2008) remarks about the ICDE Quality Review, *"ICDE reviewers attached great importance to 'learning', while the MOE focused more on 'teaching', and in fact, 'learning' has a more important role in educational activities, to which China's quality assurance standards should give more emphasis"* (p. 30).

There are also imperfections in external quality supervision, such as inadequate transparency. The government has not found out the effective ways for the release and feedback of quality supervision data, and as a result, the public has no access to complete data, or recommendations from quality reviews. Also, there is no third-party evaluation mechanism, and professionals in the distance education industry have not been able to play a major role in quality supervision. In recent years there has been some improvement, but the progress remains slow.

Open University Network

The Open University (OU) network has a profound impact on the development of distance higher education in China. It is based on the RTVU network which was formed in 1979. At that time, the population of higher education was very small. As Vice Premier Liu (2012) said, the gross enrollment ratio of higher education in 1978 was 2.7%. In order to improve access, after meeting with the then-Prime Minister of the United Kingdom Sir Edward Heath and with the experience of the Open University in the United Kingdom, the then-Vice Premier Deng Xiaoping initiated the RTVU network in China. The RTVU network was a national network, with one CRTVU in the capital city Beijing and 44 RTVUs in provinces and big cities. They worked together to offer associate degree programs of CRTVU. In 2010, to promote online flexible higher education and achieve lifelong learning for all, the central government decided to develop the OU network based on the RTVU network.

Vision and Mission

The OU network carries the responsibility to promote lifelong learning for all in China. It covers one national Open University of China and many local open universities. The OUC is operated by the central government. Since it was formally established in 2012, it has been a national platform of lifelong learning for all and led the transformation and upgrading of local RTVUs to OUs. Local open universities are regional platforms of lifelong learning for all and operated by the local governments. The OU network is dedicated to promoting the enhanced sharing of quality resources and propelling the implementation of the UNESCO "Education 2030" agenda to "ensure inclusive and equitable education".

Organizational Structure and Operational Mechanisms

The organizational structure of the OU network is similar to that of the RTVU network. It is a nationwide open education system.

The OUC is the core of the entire system. It is national-level and consists of headquarters, branches, colleges and study centers. At present, there is one headquarters in Beijing, 44 branches, more than 1000 colleges and 3000 learning centers located in different provinces, cities, counties and villages.

Local open universities are also very important to the entire system. The first five of RTVUs that have been transformed to OUs are Beijing Open University, Shanghai Open University, Jiangsu Open University, Yunnan Open University and Guangdong Open University.

The OUC (2015) and local open universities work closely with each other to promote the OU network. For example, they signed cooperation agreements and co-built the branches of the OUC. As branches, the local open universities take on the responsibilities of their respective regions and coordinate the construction of local colleges and study centers, while focusing on the main mission of the OUC and delivering the OUC programs. As independent universities, the local open universities can have their own strategic plans, enroll their own students and issue their own degrees. But up to December 2016, the overwhelming majority of the OU network had been delivering the OUC programs and conferring the OUC degrees.

It should be mentioned that the OUC is now increasing its numbers of new colleges and study centers through working with enterprises and industrial associations. From 2012 to 2016, the OUC established 11 industry and corporate colleges, including the School of Coal Mining, the School of Social Work, and the School of Logistics. In October 2017, the OUC established the first overseas study center in Zambia, in collaboration with China Nonferrous Metal Mining (Group) Co., Ltd.

Education Provision and Enrollment

The OU network offers a variety of degree and non-degree programs. In spring 2017, the OUC (2017) offers 30 bachelor programs, 109 associate degree programs and hundreds of non-degree programs. However, the OU network currently does not provide master or Ph.D. programs.

The OU network operates on a large scale in terms of student numbers. According to an OUC (2016) report, the total enrollment number of the OU network reached 3.59 million (1.05 million undergraduate students and 2.54 million associate degree students) in 2015.

The disadvantaged groups are the main target of the OU network. A report of the OUC (2017) shows that more than 70% of the students are from the grassroots level, 55% located in the central and western ethnic minority border regions. Of the OUC student population, 200,000 are rural students, 120,000 military personnel, 270,000 ethnic minority students, and 6,000 disabled students.

Educational Resources Development

One of the key characteristics of the OU network is providing quality educational resources. It works together with the conventional universities, enterprises, industries, associations and Internet companies to make and distribute educational resources to all Chinese people. The OUC (2017) established the National Digital Learning Resources Center, and cooperated with other colleges and universities, vocational institutions, and social educational institutions to establish 247 sub-centers, exploring and shaping an operational mechanism for the agglomeration, construction, and sharing of resources. By the end of 2016, the center had more than 50,000 high-quality educational resources. Besides that, to meet the fragmented learning needs of adults, the OUC (2017) has developed 30,000 free-to-use five-minute lectures at the digital library and special learning websites.

Delivery Model

For the in-depth integration of modern information technology and open and distance education, President Yang (2013) of the OUC named the delivery model of the OU network as "cloud-path-terminal" model. There is a "cloud platform" providing all the educational resources and online services, and several "paths" (satellite television network, Internet service provider, virtual private network, mobile network) delivering resources and services to various learning "terminals" (cloud classroom, television, mobile phone, computer, iPAD) for learners. For the OUC (2017), from 2012 to 2016, it has completed the construction of 314 cloud classrooms that integrate the comprehensive functions of multimedia, recording and broadcasting, as well as interactive video classrooms. The cloud classrooms have covered all the major cities in Gansu province, and the Xinjiang Uygur and Inner Mongolia Autonomous Regions, along with some other central and western regions. It also has researched and developed the "OUC Pad" and "OUC App" that have been put into pilot use among the students.

"Internet+" Degree Education

The OU network is the main provider of online higher education now in China. Shanghai Open University (2016) adopted the blended learning model and began to provide face-to-face as well as online teaching and learning services for the students. Based on the students' learning behavior and learning outcome, the OUC created a "Six-Network Integration" learner development model to ensure and enhance the quality of degree education. The six key factors to quality online education are online learning space, core curriculum, teaching team, learner support, learning assessment, and management. ICDE (2017) states that the OUC focuses on the quality of learner development and open online learning spaces for tens of thousands of teachers and millions of students, with customized services for migrant workers, college students as village officials, employees of large-scale enterprises (such as McDonalds), the disabled, military personnel and others.

Non-degree Education

With the development of the Chinese economy and society, people's learning needs have become more diversified and personalized. Degree education is unable to satisfy their needs for continuing education. The OU network also provides non-degree education opportunities and services for on-the-job staff, migrant workers, the elderly, and community residents. The leader of the group for building lifelong education system in National Education Advisory Council Mrs. Hao (2017) comments on the OU network that to provide services for lifelong learning for all is one of the most important characteristics of Chinese open universities compared with other countries' open universities. Beijing Open University (2017) developed "Lifelong Learning Platform for Capital Women" together with Beijing Women's Federation. The OUC (2017) has established an open university for the elderly, developed a website for elderly education, and planned to build a national demonstration center for health and artistic pension service experience to explore a new model of education for the elderly.

Credit Bank

As we mentioned above, the OU network provides formal and non-formal higher education programs. Since 2012 it has started to research and design a model called "Credit Bank" for the accreditation, accumulation and transfer of formal and informal learning outcomes. The OUC (2017), under the guidance of the MOE, has completed a general framework for a national credit bank system with "frame+standard" technical path, and carried out pilot work. It has organized 55 units, including relevant ministries and commissions, colleges and universities, vocational schools, open universities, training institutions and communities, to be engaged. From 2012 to 2016, more than 670 accreditation standards had been developed. An alliance for the mutual recognition of learning outcomes has been initiated and established. 67 Learning Outcome Accreditation Sub-Centers have been established across China and 4.3 million personal learning accounts have been created. The OUC (2017) launched an online platform called "Online Credit Bank Platform" on November 10, 2017. It enables millions of learners to study and transfer their learning outcomes, anywhere, anytime.

In the past five years, the OU network has made great strides in reform and development as well as capacity building. It has been recognized by the Chinese society and the world. ICDE (2017) awarded the Institutional Prize of Excellence 2017 to the OUC and praised it for its very significant achievements and contributions to the international community of open and distance education.

Future Development of Distance Higher Education

At present, there is a significant market potential for online education in China. The iResearch Company (2016) predicts that from 2013 to 2018 the market scale of online education in China will increase from 83.97 billion Yuan to 204.61 billion Yuan, with an average annual growth rate of approximately 20%.

The scale of online higher education is now expanding. The State Council of China (2014) announced its decision that the establishment of online colleges of campus-based universities is exempt from its approval and the power to approve is handed down to local governments. Now, all campus-based universities can provide online degree education if they have the approval from local governments. Furthermore, with growing personalized and diversified demands of students, the OU network will continue to play an important role in degree continuing education programs and lifelong learning for all in the future. It will continue to be a significant component of distance higher education.

Online higher education tends to blur the traditional boundary between the OU network and campus-based universities, and hence some changes have occurred in the relationship between them. The first is the tendency towards convergence. Campus-based universities have begun to implement a blended learning mode, while the OU network puts more and more emphasis on quality supervision for student support at learning centers. The second is the tendency towards competition. With more flexibility in conducting open and distance learning and growing market demand, campus-based universities have shown increasing enthusiasm for offering online education. Some of them, like Zhejiang University and Tsinghua University, have accumulated rich experience in online education, which is well connected with their campus-based offerings in terms of the delivery platform, course components and teaching faculty, thus gaining a good reputation in society. This situation poses new challenges for the OU network to build capacity and enhance quality, not only at the present time, but also in the near future. It would be advisable for the open universities and campus-based universities to find a balance between competition and collaboration. They have their own strengths and weaknesses which can compensate and complement each other in mutually beneficial ways.

The worldwide emergence of massive open online courses (MOOCs) has had a noticeable impact on distance higher education in China. For example, in 2013, Tsinghua University and Peking University joined Edx, while Fudan University and Jiaotong University joined Coursera. Furthermore, the top nine Chinese universities formed an alliance to offer "Chinese MOOCs", and enterprises—such as the Alibaba Group—have taken part in the co-creation of "Chinese MOOCs". Several universities have launched their own MOOC platforms, such as "xuetangx.com" of Tsinghua University, with an independent construction and operating model. Prompted by the MOOCs boom, in April 2015 the MOE (2015b) promulgated the *Opinions and Suggestions for Promoting the Construction, Application and Management of MOOCs*, which created favorable policy conditions for the orderly development of MOOCs.

On the other hand, several problems with distance higher education in China need to be highlighted. The quality of online education and campus education is considered to be different by policymakers, practitioners, researchers and the public. It is ingrained in people's minds that campus education is the preferred model to produce the best qualified graduates. Students who have obtained their qualifications via online education may face discrimination in employment as well as with regard to their reputation in society. Although the distance higher education sector continually strives to improve the quality of its programs and student support, it remains difficult to make significant progress. It is recommended that the institutions, policy makers and society should all contribute to enhancing its quality, by taking a holistic view. For example, policy makers should consider revising the quality standards for both open distance learning and campus-based learning, making them comparable, and also establishing sound external evaluation and monitoring mechanisms.

Despite many problems, the development prospects for distance higher education in China remain positive. The evidence of growth and demand makes it clear that the online higher education sector in China can look forward to a future of expansion to meet the needs of communities.

References

Beijing Open University. (2017). *Introduction of lifelong learning platform for capital women.* Retrieved October 20, 2017 from http://sse.bjou.edu.cn/hzxm/nxxxpt.htm.

China Internet Network Information Center. (2017). *The 40th statistical report on internet development in China.* Retrieved October 20, 2017 from http://www.cnnic.cn/hlwfzyj/hlwxzbg/hlwtjbg/201708/P020170807351923262153.pdf.

Hao, K. M. (2017). *The speech on five-year development of Open Universities in China.* Shanghai: Shanghai Open University.

ICDE. (2017). *Open University of China wins 2017 ICDE institutional prize of excellence.* Retrieved October 20, 2017 from https://www.icde.org/index.php?option=com_content&view=article&id=859:open-university-of-china-wins-2017-icde-institutional-prize-of-excellence&catid=23:news&Itemid=169&from=timeline&isappinstalled=0#sthash.lLeTC58U.X2puK54I.dpbs.

IResearch Company. (2016). *2015 China online education report.* Retrieved March 14, 2016 from http://www.jmedia360.com/news/1351.html.

Li, J. (2007). The state and appraisement of China distance education regulations. *Distance Education in China, 32*(7), 25–29.

Li, W., Yao, W. J., & Chen, N. (2014). *Strategic development for advancing ODL institutions: A SWOT analysis from the Open University of China.* Paper presented at the 28th AAOU Conference, Hong Kong.

Liu, Y. D. (2012). *To further the reform of higher education by taking a connotative development path and putting quality as the core.* Retrieved January 14, 2017 from http://www.moe.gov.cn/jyb_xwfb/moe_176/201205/t20120516_135808.html.

Ministry of Education. (1999). *Notice on launching a modern distance education pilot project for the first batch of conventional universities.* Retrieved September 14, 2016 from http://www.eblcu.cn/html/2006/4a3bc7c9375e2_0307/4561.html.

Ministry of Education. (2002). *Notice on the mid-term evaluation conclusion on the pilot program of CRTVU and 22 provincial RTVUs by the general office of the MOE.* Retrieved June 14, 2016 from http://www.moe.edu.cn/moe_879/moe_165/moe_0/moe_8/moe_30/tnull_334.html.

Ministry of Education. (2007a). *Notice on the summative evaluation on CRTVU's reform of professional training mode and pilot projects in open education by the general office of the MOE.* Retrieved June 14, 2016 from http://www.moe.gov.cn/srcsite/A07/moe_743/s3865/200711/t20071122_110619.html.

Ministry of Education. (2007b). *Notice of inspection on distance education pilot project of CRTVU and campus-based Universities by the general office of the MOE.* Retrieved June 14, 2016 from http://www.moe.gov.cn/srcsite/A07/moe_743/s3865/200712/t20071210_110612.html.

Ministry of Education. (2010). *National outline for medium and long-term education reform and development (2010–2020).* Beijing: People's Publishing Press.

Ministry of Education. (2015a). *Annual report on online colleges of campus-based Universities.* Beijing: MOE Press.

Ministry of Education. (2015b). *Opinions on strengthening university online open course construction and management application.* Beijing: People's Publishing Press.

Ministry of Education. (2016). *Education statistics 2016.* Retrieved October 20, 2017 from http://www.moe.edu.cn/s78/A03/moe_560/jytjsj_2016/.

National Bureau of Statistics. (2015). *China annual national data.* Retrieved October 20, 2017 from http://data.stats.gov.cn/english/easyquery.htm?cn=C01.

Open University of China. (2015). *Annual report 2015.* Beijing: OUC Press.

Open University of China. (2016). *New-style university.* Retrieved June 14, 2016 from http://en.ouchn.edu.cn/index.php/about-v2/new-style-university.

Open University of China. (2017). *Five-year anniversary report.* Beijing: OUC Press.

Shanghai Open University. (2016). *The development report of Shanghai Open University.* Beijing: Ministry of Education.

State Council of China. (2014). *Decision to cancel and decentralize a number of administrative approval procedures.* Retrieved March 14, 2016 from http://www.gov.cn/zwgk/2014–02/15/content_2602146.htm.

Strategic Office of CRTVU. (2010). *Education statistics yearbook of radio and TV Universities in China.* Beijing: China Central Radio and TV University Press.

Xi, J. P. (2014, February 28). To build China into a network powerhouse. *Xinhua News.* Retrieved March 14, 2016 from http://www.hn.xinhuanet.com/2014-02/28/c_119543215.htm.

Xu, H. (2008). Quality audit by ICDE: Ontological significance and academic deductions. *Distance Education in China, 27*(11), 28–32.

Yang, Z. J. (2013). The construction of National Open University: Reform and innovation. *Distance Education in China, 32*(4), 6–10.

Yang, Z. J. (2014). *Upgrade and system construction: An investigation on the Chinese radio and TV University System.* Beijing: OUC Press.

Zheng, Q. H. (2014). Learning theory and improved path of cost-effectiveness of distance education. *Open Education Research, 20*(5), 29–37.

Dr. Wei Li is an associate professor and the director of the Comparative Education Research Office at the Open University of China.

Ms. Na Chen is currently an assistant researcher in the Department of International Cooperation and Exchange at the Open University of China.

Chapter 3
China—Commentary

Jingjing Zhang

This chapter provides an inside account and perspective on higher distance education in China. The chapter unfolds in three parts—introduction to distance education in China, Chinese national open university (OU) network, future developments of distance education in China, to outline a detailed description of the changing practices of correspondence education to more open and flexible learning via the Internet.

In Part 1, opening with the history of distance education in China, the chapter progresses through its goals, mission, scale, funding sources, and finally points out the problematics of quality assurance of distance education with glimpses of the regulatory frameworks and policy supporting distance education in China. The problems rooted in both internal quality assurance and external quality supervision and evaluation were identified. The discussions of internal and external quality assurance in this part are consistent with a large body of related research concerning quality assurance of distance education. Apart from examining quality assurance from the internal and external perspectives, quality in distance education can be interpreted differently for policy makers, institutional administrators, teaching staff, and students (Jung, Wong, Li, Baigaltugs, & Belawati, 2011), many of these various problems which have occurred in quality assurance run counter to the conditions called for to meet the fast-growing demand of online provision (i.e. quantity over quality). If the directions of change to meet the challenges to be faced by distance education continue to ignore these problems, it is hard to be optimistic about the contribution of higher distance education to the discussion of widening access to higher education as well as to develop the lifelong learning society in the long run. We can only hope that efforts will be sought to make the critical policy decisions soon.

In Part 2, a rather detailed description of Chinese national OU network is presented. Given that China has the largest open and distance learning network in the world (Wei, 2010), the format spotlights the importance of the history, development

J. Zhang (✉)
Faculty of Education, Beijing Normal University, Beijing, China
e-mail: e.jingjing.zhang@gmail.com

© The Author(s) 2019
O. Zawacki-Richter and A. Qayyum (eds.), *Open and Distance Education in Asia, Africa and the Middle East*, SpringerBriefs in Open and Distance Education, https://doi.org/10.1007/978-981-13-5787-9_3

and future of Chinese OU network. Adding to the authors' discourse, I would like to further point out that China's Radio & TV Universities (RTVUs) in China have long been designated "second-class" education with high inertia, problematic goals, and disordered management, as the primary and historical mission of RTVUs is to reduce educational costs for a large number of adult learners at the college level. In this historical context, China's open universities were established to shift from their earlier mission of providing mainly second or sole chances to gain qualifications to reposition themselves to work toward a more open and flexible learner-centered learning system. They are described as "new-style" universities with Chinese characteristics and are commissioned to be open to all members of society, in order to build a knowledge economy in China and to further the international movement in distance education. The strength of open universities lies in their learning support services, which are operated primarily by online tutors (Tait, 2003). Nevertheless, newly established open universities in China have not developed the granular role definition of online tutors (Li, Zhang, Yu, & Chen, 2014). There is lack of detailed documentation on the competencies required of tutors. This missing detail poses a considerable challenge to specifying the roles of tutors, the competencies required of those roles, and the expected proficiency levels for each competency. This challenge derives from the complexity of the RTVUs system. Not only does the system entail a tier of universities, colleges, work stations, and teaching and learning centers, but the consequences are also difficult to describe and more difficult to interpret. Furthermore, the rapid reforms implemented in open universities introduce additional challenges in defining the role and its corresponding competencies. Intertwined with both traditional values and the new missions of open universities, the roles and competencies of tutors are ambiguous and contested (Li et al., 2017).

In Part 3, The problems were identified as new challenges for the future development of distance education in China, such as the competition between conventional universities and open universities to enhance their online provision and the little recognition of the quality of online learning versus traditional learning experience in higher education. Although OUs and conventional universities are to some extent different in nature, we need to situate the interpretation of their online provision under the national framework of "education informatization", which is equivalent to "ICT in Education" in a Western context. This national framework does not only provide guidance to upgrade information infrastructure in educational settings, but also puts forward the approaches to enhance education modernization, personalization, diversification, lifelong learning and internationalization (Yuan, 2013). Education informatization is seen as a strategic plan that China adopted to accelerate education modernization by implementing education informatization in all types of education at all levels. By 2020, a fundamental, informatized education system for all types of schools at all levels in the city and the countryside shall be completed so as to improve the modernization of educational resources, instructional design and teaching and learning strategies. "Internet Plus", which is proposed by premier Keqiang Li in 2015, is now widely used to create a new growth engine and to promote transformation in economic and social sectors. According to the action plan, China will push forward the integration of the Internet and education, fueling its expansion from face-to-face tuition to open and flexible online learning. On the way to meet the goal in the strategical plan of education informatization, the new "Internet Plus" policy will to a large extent boost the current online provision both in OU networks and conventional universities. Although facing great challenges that are presented in the chapter, China is now facing great opportunities to upsurge the development of distance higher education.

References

Jung, I., Wong, T. M., Li, C., Baigaltugs, S., & Belawati, T. (2011). Quality assurance in Asian distance education: Diverse approaches and common culture. *The International Review of Research in Open and Distributed Learning, 12*(6), 63–83.

Li, S., Zhang J., Yu, C., & Chen, L. (2017). *Rethinking distance tutoring in e-learning environments: A study of the priority of roles and competencies of Open University Tutors in China*. The International Review of Research in Open and Distributed Learning. (In press).

Li, S., Zhang, Y., Chen, L., Zhang, J., & Liu, Y. (2014). An empirical research on role identification and duty transformation in the era of online education. *China Educational Technology, 9*, 50–58.

Tait, A. (2003). Guest editorial—Reflections on student support in open and distance learning. *The International Review of Research in Open And Distributed Learning, 4*(1). Retrieved from http://www.irrodl.org/index.php/irrodl/article/view/134/214.

Wei, R. (2010). China's radio and TV universities: reflections on theory and practice of open and distance learning. *Open Learning: The Journal of Open, Distance and e-Learning, 25*(1), 45–56.

Yuan, G. (2013). Education in China, Beijing Normal University Press.

Chapter 4
India

Santosh Panda and Suresh Garg

Introduction

This chapter analyses the status and prospects of distance education (DE) in India. The analysis focuses on the developments so far, the direction for online and blended learning, and what careful changes are required for DE in Indian higher education and government policies. We also consider if currently unfolding scenarios will be sustainable. We include our individual experiences as well as official data and research evidence.

The National Higher Education System in India

India is a multi-cultural, plural country with the second largest population and the third largest higher education system in the world after the United States and China (Jayaram, 2007). In ancient times, it had world's largest educational system. It inherited the English education system during the British rule and, after colonial independence in 1947, embarked upon educational expansion through its Five-Year Plans. Currently, India has three types of higher education institutions: universities, colleges and stand-alone institutions. Universities can award degrees. Colleges cannot award degrees in their own name and are affiliated or recognized with universities. Stand-alone institutions offer diplomas in technical, management, nursing and teacher training programs. The expansion of higher education in the post-independence period

S. Panda (✉)
Indira Gandhi National Open University, New Delhi, India
e-mail: spanda.ignou@gmail.com

S. Garg
Usha Martin University, Ranchi, India

© The Author(s) 2019
O. Zawacki-Richter and A. Qayyum (eds.), *Open and Distance Education in Asia, Africa and the Middle East*, SpringerBriefs in Open and Distance Education, https://doi.org/10.1007/978-981-13-5787-9_4

has been tremendous. In 1951 there were 30 universities and 7000 colleges (University Grants Commission (UGC), 2013). Currently, in 2018 there are 903 universities, 39,050 colleges and 10,011 stand-alone institutions, serving 36.6 million students (Ministry of Human Resource Development (MHRD), 2018, p. 1). Even in recent years, the growth has been notable. In 2012 there were 700 universities and six years later, there are over 900 universities.

There are six categories of universities and university-level institutions in India: central universities, state public universities, deemed universities, state private universities, institutes of national importance and institutes under the state act. Central universities have been established by the national government of India, while state universities are run and funded by state governments. "Deemed" universities have autonomy from the governments but are public institutions. Private universities are approved by the University Grants Commission. Institutes of national importance include premier higher education institutions focusing mainly, though not exclusively, on engineering, information technology, medicine, and other sciences. Institutes under the State Act for instance are medical science institutes established by the State Legislature Act. There are 15 open universities (OUs) dedicated to distance education, one of which, the Indira Gandhi National Open University is a central university and the other 14 are state universities. Open and distance learning (ODL) is also offered at conventional (dual-mode) universities as well as by stand-alone ODL institutions like the OUs.

History and Status of Distance and Online Education

After independence in 1947, India had to face the challenge of providing access to higher education to cover growing number of youth and disadvantaged sections of society. The working population also felt an increasing need for continuing professional development. However, there were limits on expanding the formal system due to paucity of funds. The Third Five Year Plan (1961–67) of the Government of India (Government of India (GoI), 1961) emphasized the expansion of physical and other teaching facilities to match increased demand with increasing student enrolments. The plan recommended considering evening colleges and correspondence courses, and awarding external degrees.

Subsequently, a senior team from the University Grants Commission (UGC) visited the Soviet Union to study their system of correspondence education and evening classes. In 1961, the Central Advisory Board of Education (the highest government educational policy-making body) recommended establishment of a committee under the chairmanship of the UGC to examine the matter. The committee's report of 1963 recommended the following:

A correspondence course should be a step designed to expand and equalize educational opportunity, as it aimed at providing additional opportunities for several thousand students who wished to continue their education and the persons who had been denied these facilities and were in full-time employment or were for other reasons prevented from availing themselves of the facilities at college. (Government of India (GoI), 1963, pp. 3–4)

Correspondence education at the undergraduate level was initiated in 1962 at the premier University of Delhi with 1112 arts students on an experimental basis (Panda, 2005). The comprehensive Kothari Education Commission of 1964–66 strongly recommended part-time and own-time (or self-study) education through programs such as evening colleges and correspondence courses respectively. Since then, the system of continuing education (CE) has expanded, with premier universities establishing directorates or departments of correspondence education.

With pressure from international developments in lifelong learning (Panda, 2011) and internal pressure and efforts by educational leaders, the first (provincial) open university was established in India in 1982, in the erstwhile state of unified Andhra Pradesh. It is now called the Dr. B. R. Ambedkar Open University. The Indira Gandhi National Open University (IGNOU) was mandated in 1985 by an Act of Parliament. Along with the national open university, there are now 14 state funded provincial open universities, with the latest one established in 2015 in the state of Odisha:

- Dr. B. R. Ambedkar Open University—1982
- Nalanda Open University—1987
- Vardhaman Mahaveer Open University—1987
- Yashwantrao Chavan Maharashtra Open University—1989
- Madhya Pradesh Bhoj Open University—1991
- Dr. Babasaheb Ambedkar Open University—1994
- Karnataka State Open University—1996
- Netaji Subhas Open University—1997
- Uttar Pradesh Rajarshi Tandon Open University—1999
- Tamil Nadu Open University—2002
- Uttarakhand Open University—2005
- Pandit Sundarlal Sharma Open University—2005
- Krishna Kanta Handiqui State Open University—2006
- Odisha State Open University—2015.

IGNOU was assigned the dual responsibility of being an open university and acting as a national nodal agency (in a way, as a regulator) to promote, coordinate and accredit distance education systems and programs in the country. The DE system expanded quickly 1985 after (Table 4.1).

Dual mode DE is offered by central universities, state universities, deemed universities, state private universities and institutions of national importance. Stand-alone institutions offering ODL include professional associations, government institutions, private institutions. Dual-mode universities programs were required to follow the same syllabus and exams of the parent university to maintain parity with the parent university, except that the delivery mode was different. In many cases such institutes were milch cows for the main university. The establishment of single-mode

Table 4.1 Growth of ODL institutions

Year	Conventional universities	Correspondence institutes at conventional universities	Open universities	Total institutions offering DE
1962–63	61	1		1
1967–68	80	3	–	3
1975–76	115	22	–	22
1982–83	134	34	1	35
1985–86	151	38	2	40
1990–91	190	46	5	51
2000–01	256	70	9	79
2004–05	343	104	11	117
2009–10	532	183	14	250
2013–14	666	198	14	264

Source Quoted from Indira Gandhi National Open University (IGNOU) (2016)

open universities, especially IGNOU, brought about significant reforms, including the following:

- Pressuring and guiding dual-mode institutions to improve quality in terms of curriculum, self-learning materials, use of ICT, learner support, and assessment and evaluation;
- Initiating new national and regional development programs and continuing professional development/training programs in open universities;
- Initiating reforms in curriculum and instructional design with credit-based and modular courses, integration of ICT in teaching and learning, extended networks of tutors and course writer academics, and learner-based student support services;
- Developing and digitizing of a vast amount of learning resources (print, audio, video, interactive multimedia, teleconferencing, PowerPoint, etc.) (Panda, 1999) through a national resource repository, today known as OER—open educational resources;
- Providing a network of facilities such as teleconferencing centers, satellite studios, well-trained educational media professionals, and a national satellite dedicated to education and training;
- Enabling accreditation and quality assurance mechanisms in the DE system and programs through the statutory Distance Education Council (DEC) of IGNOU.

Combining OUs and dual-mode institutions, enrollments in ODL have been growing substantially (Table 4.2). Government of India data from the Eleventh five-year plan (2007–2012) stated there were 1.77 million ODL student enrollments in open universities and 2.42 ODL student enrollments outside of OUs. This calculates to just over 4.2 million ODL students, which is 16.1% of the total of 25.99 million higher

Table 4.2 ODL enrollment growth

Year	Enrolment in conventional universities	Enrolment in open universities	Enrolment in ODL other than OUs
1967–68	1,370,261	–	8577
1975–76	2,426,109	–	64,210
1982–83	3,133,093	–	197,555
1985–86	3,605,029	17,009	355,090
1990–91	4,924,868	102,820	592,814
2000–01	8,399,443	623,892	1,378,000
2004–05	11,038,543	886,612	2,124,591
2009–10	17,243,352	1,630,392	2,140,000
2011–12	25,990,000	1,777,000	2,424,000

Source DEC Databases as quoted from Indira Gandhi National Open University (IGNOU) (2016), *New Education Policy 2015*: *Outcome Document*). n.a. = not available; Government of India (GOI) (2013)

education student enrollments. For the twelfth five-year plan, (2012–2017) the governments' goal was to increase ODL to 5.2 million students out of a total of 35.9 million higher education students, by 2017. Historically ODL enrollments outside of OUs have been a larger percentage of OL students than within OUs. However, enrollments within open universities seem to be growing at a faster rate than ODL outside of OUs.

ICT and Distance Education

With the initiation of correspondence education in 1962, radio (and, later on, audio) enabled provision of supplementary learning resources to the students. Television was added only after the 1975 Satellite Instructional Television Experiment (SITE) in agricultural and community education, along with Farm Radio. In 1984 the UGC started the 'Countrywide Classroom' television and video series. It was produced by means of a network of university media centers and broadcast through the government national television network *Doordarshan*. Distance education received a boost in 2005 with the launch of a dedicated satellite for education (EduSat), with the aim of expanding 'dialogue and interaction'. The use of ICT in the sub-continent has kept pace with global trends, including their application to education and training. However, the school sector has experimented with and deployed technology developments faster and more widely than the higher education sector (Chaudhary & Panda, 2005).

Three types of distance and online learning delivery systems are available in India:

(i) Traditional distance learning delivery, using print materials (self-learning), with learner support provided by part-time study centers;

(ii) Multimedia courseware, with learner support provided by both study centers and online;

(iii) Fully online delivery of programs—learning resources, activities and assignments, synchronous and asynchronous interaction, online support, and online assessment.

Single-mode OUs and only a few dual-mode university "Distance Education Institutes" (also called distance education units) have been able to develop multimedia-based instructional design models. IGNOU has developed a model of credit-based instructional design whereby each component of teaching and learning (including ICT) forms part of the credit system, in a modular learning design. This framework was adopted by provincial open universities and the majority of dual-mode universities, through the Distance Education Council (DEC). The DEC had the mandate to provide government funding to distance education institutions, and required inclusion of ICT in instructional design as a pre-condition to funding.

IGNOU offered many online programs through largely the Moodle learning management system. As many as 42 academic programs were till recently offered online. In the process of technology design and deployment for teaching and learning, IGNOU embarked upon the contemporary version of 'blended learning', in combination with OERs. The best example is the award-winning postgraduate diploma in e-learning (Panda, 2013). The instructional strategy combines independent study, lectures, discussions, group work, collaborative learning, role play and a project (Mythili, 2015).

The expansion of online learning clearly requires a concomitant expansion of broadband connectivity. Internet penetration in India was at 27% of the total population as of 2016, with 335 million internet users. Further, 4G broadband connectivity for mobile phone services is expanding fast, and the number of users was expected to grow to 72% of the population by 2016. A survey by the *Times of India* newspaper in 2012 (Ahmed & Garg, 2015) showed that internet access at that time was 90% from computers, 48% from mobile phones and 11% from tablets. The worldwide market for e-learning is set to grow to $51 billion by 2016, with a 5-year compound annual growth rate of 7.6% (for India the growth rate is estimated to be 17.4%).

Many e-learning companies have created a complete package including an online learning platform, learning resources, interaction and assessment mechanisms. Many colleges, universities and particularly secondary schools, have adopted such a package in order to offer exclusive online programs, or to provide supplementary academic support to students. Simultaneously, we have seen the entry of international free-of-cost, open content providers such as the Khan Academy, EdX and Coursera, which have ambitious plans to tap into the Indian e-learning and e-training markets. However, e-learning is not growing as fast as the e-commerce sector in the country. One reason for this could be the traditional cultural mindset of the population which prefers individual and book/lecture-based learning, and also their lack of faith in network-based knowledge sharing (Santosh & Panda, 2016).

Formulating a national policy on ICT in education has been difficult and there is still no national policy exclusively for the use of ICT in higher education. The National Policy on Information Technology (NPIT) was adopted by the Indian Government in 2001. It aimed to decentralize, empower, and develop skilled human resources for the IT sector. The National Policy on Information and Communication Technology in School Education (NPICTSE) was formulated in 2012. This was the culmination of many earlier ICT developments in the school sector including the CLASS project (computers in schools in 1984), interactive multimedia on hardspots for school education under the Sarva Shiksha Abiyan/Education For All movement, and mobile learning in schools with subsidized *Aakash* tablet computers (supposedly the cheapest tablet in the world).

In parallel, there have been developments in technologies and networks in India, which have eventually come to support distance and online learning (Commonwealth of Learning (COL), 2015):

- In 1996 The INFLIBNET (information and library network center) was established to network all libraries in higher education.
- Community-based multipurpose tele-learning centers were established (Panda & Chaudhary, 2001).
- In 2005 the National Knowledge Network was established to provide high-speed broadband connectivity to all education and training institutions, free of cost.
- In 2006, the National Electronic Knowledge Repository (*E-Gyankosh*) of IGNOU was established and was put into the open domain in 2008.
- The National Mission on Education through ICT offered free, interactive curriculum-based digital content on the open source portal *Sakshat* (now based at SWAYAM).
- The National E-Library provides quality, free digital content from premier higher education institutions.
- The National Repository of Open Educational Resources (NROER) for school education was established by the National Council for Educational Research and Training.
- The *E-PG-Pathsala* (electronic classroom) program of the UGC funds institutions of higher learning to develop digital e-content (to finally be housed at the national platform of SWAYAM).
- 'Digital India' was launched—this is the flagship initiative of the present National Democratic Alliance government to make the entire country digitally literate and empowered.
- The Indian Government launched SWAYAM—the Study Webs of Active-Learning for Young Aspiring Minds, which is an online MOOC-based national portal for free, credit-based content delivery (quoted in Business Standard, 2017a).

Funding of Distance Education

The funding of higher education institutions in the country are diverse and difficult. The central universities and institutions of national importance are fully funded by the central government, mainly through the UGC. IGNOU is directly, though not fully, funded by the central government, and does not fall under the UGC for direct funding or for regulation/accreditation (though its regulation and accreditation by UGC through DEB is a recent development). State universities, including state open universities, are funded by state governments (with developmental grants from the UGC, if eligible). The deemed-to-be universities are variously funded (but generally by private initiatives). Private universities and colleges fund their own expenses. The dual-mode university DEIs are funded by the parent university.

Education is in the concurrent imperatives of the Indian Constitution, so both central and state governments have stakes and need to fund education, including higher education. In 1995–96, the share of central government in plan and non-planned expenditures on higher education was 51.51 and 11.46% respectively. Planned expenditures are activity-based, therefore variable, while non-planned expenditures are assured and fixed for given activities. Within the total education expenditure, the share of higher education plan was 6% and non-plan 11.5% (10% in total for higher education). Within non-plan expenditure, the highest proportion (i.e. 94.5%) was in the school sector, and only 76% was allocated to higher education (the rest—24%—was divided equally between endowments and fee incomes).

The liberalization of economy in the 1990s, and subsequent encouragement to privatize higher education, helped increase the percentage of the fee income component within the total expenditure figure. However, government expenditure on higher education has stabilized at about 75%, while the fee share has decreased and stabilized at about 12%. Within institutional expenditure, more than 95% is allocated to salaries for faculty and other staff, and the meager rest is available for maintenance and further development.

Open universities have, by and large, achieved economies of scale while maintaining quality. Dual-mode university DEIs spend comparatively less on DE students and in fact earn a surplus at times, which funds the parent university departments. State OUs and dual-mode university DEIs are part-funded by the central government through the Distance Education Council (located at UGC as a bureau).

State open universities are autonomous regarding decision making about program offerings and innovations in teaching and learning. They initially used learning materials from IGNOU, and subsequently developed their own self-learning materials in regional languages. These open universities gain income from four sources: grants from state government, developmental grants from central government/UGC, private grants, and student fees. For instance, the Dr. B. R. Ambedkar Open University (BRAOU), which was awarded full subsidy from the state government when it was established in 1982, now generates resources from student fees (25%), state government grants (22%), and the rest of its resources are central grants from the DEC/IGNOU. It was difficult for this first open university in the country to be economically viable, since it was spending almost 20% more on students than the resources it generated. On the other hand, as per its mandate and agreement, the Yashwantrao Chavan Maharashtra Open University (YCMOU) received a block grant each year from the state government to meet developmental costs, and was required to meet operational costs itself. As per that agreement, the YCMOU is now able to meet cent percent of its recurring expenses (after five years of existence).

An earlier study by Datt and Gaba (2006) reports that the sources of income for open universities are still mainly based on student fees:

- Yashwantrao Chavan Maharashtra Open University: student fees (90.11%), state government (7.33%), DEC/IGNOU (2.56%). (Fees as % of unit cost: 103.19).
- Dr B. R. Ambedkar Open University: student fees (82.23%), state government (17.77%). (Fees as % of unit cost: 82.23).
- Uttar Pradesh Rajarshi Tandon Open University: student fees (71.43%), state government (22.86%), DEC/IGNOU (5.71%). (Fees as % of unit cost: 123.27).
- Indira Gandhi National Open University: student fees (71.31%), central government (28.69%). (Fees as % of unit cost: 71.32).

The above data shows that some open universities charge more fees per student than their expenditure per unit. This may mean that there is a compromise in terms of quality of teaching and learning, and student learning experiences. Data from private universities and private distance education providers are not available to draw conclusions in that sector. However, personal experience of the authors shows that, barring a few who are conscious of overall quality of their provision, most private providers aim at making a profit. They either strictly economize on infrastructure and recurring expenses, or on the quality of education, or they charge higher student fees, or all of these.

While the regulator DEC was part of IGNOU, the national open university channeled grants to other DE providers and also regulated/accredited them. Although the government shifted the DEC to come under the control of UGC in 2013, IGNOU has not sacrificed its autonomy in terms of direct central funding. In 1985–86, IGNOU received full subsidy from the central government. In the following year, student fees constituted 1.86% of its income. Today student fees contribute about 75% of income, and the government contribution is 15%. Income from other sources has increased, such as the sale of publications, interest on bank deposits, and endowments.

The funding of higher education and DE in India is not based on any particular policy. Kulandai Swamy (2002) had remarked:

> Either at the time of establishing the IGNOU or later, the Government of India has not articulated a unique funding policy for the open university as such, distinct from the policy followed in funding of conventional universities. Generally, the analysis of costs and benefits of university education has not been attempted ... It is only in recent years that economics of higher education has come to be discussed and the universities are asked to generate funds. (p. 64)

A cost analysis and funding mechanism should be undertaken for both public and private DE providers. Either the central government or the DEB should develop a uniform funding system for all DE providers. This will facilitate decisions regarding the costs of online learning programs, student fees, and sources of funding. A successful resolution to the funding issue will determine the future expansion of online learning too.

Regulation, Accreditation and Quality Assurance

When IGNOU was established in 1985, the correspondence education programs in dual-mode universities were partly funded and quality assured by UGC. A conference of vice-chancellors was organized by UGC in 1990 to discuss the future and regulation of correspondence/distance education. As a result, UGC and IGNOU agreed to establish the Distance Education Council (DEC) at IGNOU as per the IGNOU Act. They decided that while IGNOU should manage the DE system (i.e. open universities), UGC would continue to control continuing education (CE) programs in the dual-mode universities and deemed universities. The DEC exercised three roles—promotional activities, coordination and maintenance of standards, and financial support.

In 1995, DEC started recognizing DE programs offered by dual-mode public universities, although online programs were not conceived within this regulation framework. Guidelines were developed for establishing DE institutions, together with their functioning regarding offering academic programs. However, since the DEC was not created by means of an Act of Parliament, it did not have legally tenable Regulations, Norms and Standards for various programs. Therefore, it began as an advisory body, providing only guidelines. Subsequently, in 2003 DEC embarked on program evaluations for formal recognition, and five years thereafter it started offering provisional institutional recognition through a coordination committee comprising nominees from UGC, AICTE and DEC. However, the chairperson of DEC was always the chairman of the joint committee.

Statute 28 of the IGNOU Act (dealing with DEC at IGNOU) was repealed by the President of India (i.e. the Visitor of the University). In 2013 DEC was placed under UGC as its Distance Education Bureau (DEB). Since then, DEB has been allowing annual and 2–5 yearly recognition of programs of all DE providers including IGNOU, and has of late formulated regulations separately for DE and online learning which have been implemented.

Territorial jurisdiction has been a matter of contention regarding DE institutions vis-à-vis campus-based universities. Due to government laws, campus-based dual-mode universities were restricted to offer DE programs within their university jurisdictional operation in a particular state, whereas state OUs had the mandate to cover the entire state. IGNOU was mandated to cover the entire country and offer programs overseas. The central universities (which are usually unitary in nature without any affiliated colleges) could accept DE students from any part of the country. These issues are now under consideration, as clear-cut policy for cross-border education begins to evolve.

Issues, Concerns and the Future

India has the largest higher education demographic globally. The gross enrollment ratio—the number of students in higher education from the possible pool from the population—was 8.1% in 2001–02 (9.3% male, 6.7% female), increasing to 21.1% in 2012–13 (22.3% male, 19.8% female). The gross enrollment ratio was 26% in 2017, with over 35 million higher education students. It is expected to be 30% by 2020. This is putting pressure on the system to expand faster than ever before. There is a need to strengthen alternative routes such as distance and online learning to provide access to education and especially skills training.

Private initiatives in education and low-cost DE, coupled with stringent quality monitoring, could address the need for more education and training opportunities, especially as public expenditure on education is not commensurate with educational need. Information and Communication Technologies (ICTs) can play a major role in expanding opportunities and provision. The Indian education sector is a lucrative market for investment. Private providers of higher education include both private institutions in India and foreign providers. Foreign direct investment in education, which was about 8.8 million rupees ($135,000 USD) in 2002–03, increased to 10 billion rupees (153 million USD) in 2008–09. But it got reduced to 1.5 billion rupees (23 million USD) in 2011–12. The number of private higher education institutions has grown phenomenally in recent decades, following the post-1990s liberalization of the Indian economy (FICCI, 2011). This is certainly going to increase in future. Though 100% foreign direct investment in education is allowed through the automatic route, private universities and colleges generally focus on professional programs with no overseas elite university actually establishing any campus in India so far (Ahmed & Garg, 2015).

Cross-border education continues to be a major challenge in terms of policy and practice. It is not healthy to allow the current 'brain drain' phenomenon to continue. The best talent in the country has been migrating to developed countries for higher study and eventually gaining employment abroad. Retaining talent in-country is a major concern.

In this context, Garg (2015) summarized the status of distance and open education in India as follows:

> … the Open Universities (OUs) are now facing Herculean challenges, which have emanated from non-recognition of their degrees for higher education and non-acceptability of graduates in the job market, low success rates/retention and high dropout rate, the demands of lifelong learning (L-3), ignorance of the purists among the intelligentsia about techniques and processes and methodologies used by open educators, rapid changes taking place within the system and criticism by different regulators. (p. 6)

The DE system is operating without a well-formulated separate national DE policy. Additional challenges that the DE system has to deal with include a government culture that is non-responsive, bureaucratic and politically active. Moreover, the under-performance that is plaguing the mainstream education system is crippling creativity and affecting quality. The ODL system is now a prisoner to this tendency.

These challenges, coupled with instability in the placement of the regulator of distance education in the national educational policy landscape, are poised to affect the future of distance and open learning.

The use of ICT continues to be a problematic area. Learning technologies are not an integral part of the pedagogic and delivery systems in either open and dual-mode universities, nor conventional institutions. Early during the development of OUs, the use of technology was significant (though supplementary) and seriously implemented, particularly since the institutions controlled the ICT-basket—print, audio, video, radio, TV, multimedia, and (tele) conferencing media. However, impediments in integrating ICTs into ODL have been created in the light of recent developments such as the semantic web, OERs, MOOCs and open source technologies. Even after 57 years of initiation of correspondence/distance education, ICT still remains as supplementary within programme design and delivery. The impediments include lack of both national and institutional policies and frameworks, academic resistance to rapid change, and high costs and resource crunch. Further, the absence of a 'system' of technology-enabled ODL inhibits distance and online learners in their individual and group learning.

ICT challenges for ODL need to be addressed in a systematic manner. This would entail:

- appropriate technology deployment, practically accessible and usable by the students;
- significant training and professional development of faculty on pedagogical integration of ICTs (Markauskaite & Goodyear, 2009);
- strategic policy and organizational realignment including policy for plural and blended pedagogic and ODL models (Arinto, 2016);
- removing barriers to effective use of ICTs in teaching and learning, and learner support;
- cost-effectiveness analysis and adoption of appropriate and economically viable strategies for program development and delivery.

Any large-scale adoption of e-learning needs to be embedded in national and institutional policy frameworks. In a study on the National Open University, Panda and Mishra (2007) reported significant barriers to e-learning as perceived by faculty, namely: access to technology and training on e-learning, institutional policy, and instructional design for e-learning. Santosh and Panda (2016) reported faculty preference for colleagues and publishing, rather than sharing in social and professional networks (and the absence of organizational recognition and incentives). This is notwithstanding the fact that a study of learner preferences suggested a preference for web-based learning, supported by print and some form of online and/or face-to-face interaction; and such an offering could be further facilitated by email and interactive multimedia support (Dikshit, Gaba, Bhushan, Garg, & Panda, 2003). In terms of pedagogic effectiveness, interactive multimedia CD-ROMs with a variety of learning activities were found to be more effective than print with face-to-face learner support and/or web-based learning with online learner support (Dikshit et al., 2013). A recent study (Panda & Santosh, 2017) underlined faculty preference for open sharing, institutional policy on OER, and continuing professional development in copyright, IPR and OER. All these issues need to be addressed early.

For a long time, there had been lack of a national credit policy in higher education, although IGNOU and other open and dual-mode universities adopted a standardized system of credits in the form of modular-based learning. The credit-based system of education and training propelled the development of national Choice-Based Credit System (CBCS) by the University Grants Commission for both campus-based and open universities and colleges in 2015. Now, all the universities are required to re-engineer their practices and shift to these national standards, although the details are still being refined. The credits system becomes complicated while considering the national online platform (SWAYAM). While universities are being encouraged to develop and use interactive, credit-based multimedia courseware for the SWAYAM platform at no charge to students, it is not clear how universities (especially open universities) will award credit for online diploma and degree programs, both within and outside the country vis-a-vis the national online platform. The existing pedagogic comprehensiveness and effectiveness of SWAYAM are being questioned when compared to some of the current good practices globally.

Both systemic and disciplinary research has long been a weak link in DE in India. In the initial years of correspondence DE, research was not a priority for academic administrators. Individuals however continued to publish research, but a research policy was only put in place in most OUs around 2000. In single mode OUs, qualifications in DE as well as publications in DE theory and practice are now held in high esteem in terms of faculty recruitment and promotion. However, DE faculty in dual-mode universities had to comply with policies meant for the parent university. Though many faculty members conducted research in their subject discipline, this was rare for DE policy and practice.

As mentioned earlier, UGC is the regulator for higher education, including research programs and policies. Its policies about DE and research in open universities have been fluid and indecisive. As a result, OUs and dual-mode universities began to deviate from rules and regulations intended for campus-based universities (including compulsory full-time credit-based coursework). For example, in 2008 IGNOU established 100 doctoral fellowship programs in all disciplines, including distance education. More than 400 full-time doctoral students pursued research in various disciplines. Then in 2009 UGC issued a notification banning M.Phil. and Ph.D. programs via distance learning. The embargo resulted in a cessation of doctoral work through distance and online learning. This is bound to affect the quality of online and DE over time, as it will become increasingly difficult to attract and retain talent. It was ironic that campus-based universities may pursue full-time doctoral work on any area of DE, yet those who have day-to-day systemic experience in distance teaching and learning are banned from conducting research in this area. This got resolved in 2017, and doctoral research at OUs and DEIs was allowed again in these institutions.

UGC continues to view DE as lacking in quality, more so in case of online learning. Even if distance education captures a sizeable proportion of higher education space, questions relating to parity of esteem and employability are still raised by higher education administrators, the judiciary and employers. In this context, leadership within DE matters. This notwithstanding, it is unfortunate that, in spite of strict guidelines being issued in 2015 regarding adherence to quality standards and scrutiny, online learning programs (at certificate, diploma and degree level) had been banned in the country as an interim measure. Since then, universities, including national and state open universities, have been constrained by not being allowed to offer academic programs online (though now the online learning regulation 2018 by UGC is under implementation). The National Education Policy 2016 (Ministry of Human Resource Development (MHRD), 2016) has been formulated, but is under national and regional consultation. It has proposed: the creation of a national agency as the regulator in the area of ODL; allowing IGNOU to offer online programs in areas including select professional areas; provided the guidelines on standards promulgated by various higher education regulators; (in fields of agriculture, law, teacher education, etc.) are adhered to; establishing and operating internal quality assurance cell by IGNOU; and carrying out an independent external evaluation of IGNOU. The Government of India is expected to pilot the Distance Education Council of India (DECI) Bill through the Indian Parliament to establish the DECI (distance education council of India) as an independent statutory regulator with sufficient mandate to impose, monitor, recognize and accredit all distance education programs (including online learning programs) in the country.

References

Ahmed, F., & Garg, S. (2015). *Higher education in knowledge era: Innovation, excellence and values*. New Delhi: Viva Books.

Arinto, P. (2016). Issues and challenges in open and distance e-learning: Perspectives from the Philippines. *International Review of Research in Open and Distance Learning, 17*(2), 162–180.

Business Standard. (2017, July 10). President of India attends the launch of SWAYAM, Swayan Prabha DTH channels & National Academic Depository. *Business Standard*.

Business Standard. Citation of five year plans.

Chaudhary, S., & Panda, S. (2005). Educational television and teleconference. In U. V. Reddi & S. Mishra (Eds.), *Educational Media in Asia*. Vancouver: The Commonwealth of Learning.

Commonwealth of Learning (COL). (2015). *A baseline study on technology-enabled learning in the Asian Commonwealth*. Vancouver: The Commonwealth of Learning.

Datt, R., & Gaba, A. (2006). Cost of dual mode and single mode distance education. In S. Garg, et al. (Eds.), *Four decades of distance education in India*. New Delhi: Viva Books.

Dikshit, J., Gaba, A., Bhushan, S., Garg, S., & Panda, S. (2003). Learning attitude, motivation and preferences of online learners. *Indian Journal of Open Learning, 12*(3).

Dikshit, J., Garg, S., & Panda, S. (2013). Pedagogic effectiveness of print, interactive multimedia and online resources: A case study of IGNOU. *International Journal of Instruction, 6*(2), 193–210.

FICCI. (2011). *Private sector participation in Indian Higher Education*. New Delhi: Federation of Indian Chamber of Commerce & Industry.

Garg, S. (2015). Open universities: Swimming against the tide. *University News, 53*(31), 6–15.

Government of India (GoI). (1961). *Third five-year plan*. New Delhi: Planning Commission, Government of India.

Government of India (GoI). (1963). *Report of the expert committee on correspondence courses*. New Delhi: Ministry of Education, Government of India.

Government of India (GOI). (2013). *Twelfth five year plan (2012–2017): Social sectors* (Vol. III). New Delhi: Sage.

IGNOU. (2016). *New education policy 2015: Outcome document.* New Delhi: Indira Gandhi National Open University.

Jayaram, N. (2007). India. In J. F. Forest, P. Altbach, & G. Philip (Eds.), *International handbook of higher education, Part Two: Regions and countries.* Singapore: Springer.

Kulandai Swamy, V. C. (2002). Open and distance learning, and concerns of access and equity. In H. P. Dikshit, S. Garg, S. Panda, & Vijayshri (Eds.), *Access and equity: Challenges for open and distance learning.* New Delhi: Kogan Page.

Markauskaite, L., & Goodyear, P. (2009). *Designing for complex ICT-based learning.* Paper Presented at the 26th Annual Conference of ASCILITE, Auckland, New Zealand.

Ministry of Human Resource Development (MHRD). (2016). *National Policy on Education 2016: Report of the committee for evolution of the new education policy.* New Delhi: Government of India.

Ministry of Human Resource Development (MHRD). (2018). *All India Survey on Higher Education 2017–18.* New Delhi: Government of India.

Mythili, G. (2015). India Gandhi National Open University—OER-based postgraduate diploma in e-learning. In S. Naidu & S. Mishra (Eds.), *Case studies on OER-based e-learning.* New Delhi: Commonwealth Educational Media Centre for Asia.

Panda, S. (1999). Developments, networking and convergence in India. In K. Harry (Ed.). *Higher education through open and distance learning* (pp. 199–212). London & New York: Routledge & COL.

Panda, S. (2005). Higher education at a distance and national development: Reflections on the Indian experience. *Distance Education, 26*(2), 205–225.

Panda, S. (2011). Continuing education and lifelong learning in the Indian sub-continent: Critical reflections. *International Journal of Continuing Education and Lifelong Learning, 4*(1), 25–48.

Panda, S. (2013). Innovation in ICT application for education and training: Postgraduate diploma in e-learning. In S. Santosh & C. K. Ghosh (Eds.), *Creative sparks of innovation.* New Delhi: Indira Gandhi National Open University.

Panda, S., & Chaudhary, S. (2001). Telelearning and telelearning centers in India. In C. Latchem & D. Walker (Eds.), *Telecenters: Case studies and key issues.* Vancouver: The Commonwealth of Learning.

Panda, S., & Mishra, S. (2007). E-learning in a mega open university: Faculty attitude, barriers and motivators. *Educational Media International, 44*(4), 323–338.

Panda, S., & Santosh, S. (2017). Faculty perception of openness and attitude to open sharing at the Indian National Open University. *International Review of Research in Open and Distributed Learning, 18*(7), 89–111.

Santosh, S., & Panda, S. (2016). Sharing of knowledge among faculty in a Mega Open University. *Open Praxis, 8*(3), 247–264.

University Grants Commission (UGC). (2013). *Higher Education in India at a Glance.* New Delhi: University Grants Commission.

Chapter 5
India—Commentary

Ramesh Chander Sharma

Distance education (DE) in India can be considered as a good showcase of all generations of DE which have been identified by scholars like Jim Taylor, Tony Bates, Terry Anderson. Starting with the establishment of the School of Correspondence Courses and Continuing Education at Delhi University in 1962, it has come a long way riding the MOOC wave by imparting courses through SWAYAM (Study Webs of Active Learning for Young Aspiring Minds)—an initiative of the Government of India (https://swayam.gov.in/) for providing opportunities for life-long learning. Distance education has covered all levels of education: primary, secondary, and higher tertiary and various disciplines from general to professional and technical in nature. The canvas of distance education in India is quite big, with having One National Open University, more than 15 State Open Universities as single mode universities, dual mode universities offering DE programs, National Institute of Open Schooling along with State Open Schools catering for school education, and private institutions etc.

The changing nature of DE has resulted in its management too. Distance Education Council (DEC) was established as a Regulatory Body, initially with Indira Gandhi National Open University, later on taken over by University Grants Commission. In addition, there are other regulatory bodies for technical, management, health and law etc. This has results in discussions and confusion over the jurisdiction of universities offering courses, which course can and cannot be offered by distance mode. To give a proper direction to the system in the country, work on National Educational Policy is in progress and ODL need to be an integral to this national policy. The DE system is facing the challenge of leadership with various open universities in different phases of development.

The role of open universities becomes very important in this current 4th Industrial Revolution when various sectors, industries, economies are being impacted by

R. C. Sharma (✉)
Ambedkar University Delhi, New Delhi, India
e-mail: rc_sharma@yahoo.com

© The Author(s) 2019
O. Zawacki-Richter and A. Qayyum (eds.), *Open and Distance Education in Asia,
Africa and the Middle East*, SpringerBriefs in Open and Distance Education,
https://doi.org/10.1007/978-981-13-5787-9_5

new technologies. The emergence of artificial intelligence, gamification, virtual and augmented reality, internet of things, micro-learning etc. are some of the technologies and trends already in place and use in industries like manufacturing, banking, transport, telecommunications etc. Education or Distance Education cannot remain aloof from these developments and thus following challenges needs to be taken care of at the earliest:

Learning paradigms/designs: With traditional jobs disappearing fast and new job roles emerging, it is pertinent to design courses and learning experiences which would enhance the digital literacy of learners. According to the predictions of World Economic Forum, by the year 2020, around 35% of the skills used in current market settings will change drastically. The learning designers for ODL courses (the course materials changed from being printed text to self-instructional to self-learning materials) need to plan for developing skills like complex problem solving, critical thinking, and cognitive flexibility etc.

Pedagogy: With various pedagogical models like cognitive or behavioristic or constructivist, Indian ODL system need to focus on how we can prepare our learner as creators of knowledge. Modern learners live, learn and work in a digital society. There is a need for new set of academic and professional practices to support their digital behavior, practices and identities. Perhaps the "Digital and Information Literacy Framework" of the UKOU can be a good lead for Indian Open Universities.

Recognition of Learning and acquired skills: Government of India launched SWAYAM, a MOOC platform. There are many other self learning platforms available from where learners enroll in the courses of their liking and interest. A mechanism needs to be put in place where such learning is given value or recognition for further admission to a program or employment.

Student support: E-commerce companies have changed the way the customer services can be successfully accomplished. The digital society needs different mechanisms and operations to provide services to its learners. The modern distance learner is 'always connected', thus academic or administrative support for ODL learners appropriate processes and products like we note services provided through Internet of Things enabled devices, robots and artificial intelligence applications.

Openness: There is a need to examine the extent of openness the system is following. This may be in terms of content, admissions, program offerings, pedagogy, technology, assessment and accreditation etc.

Accountability, Regulations and Quality Assurance: Currently there are challenges of coordination, jurisdiction, delivery and the nature of courses to be offered through ODL in the country. Various regulatory authorities add to this chaos. Differing policy decisions lead to confusion among learners, institutions and other stake holders. What can or cannot go in for general education, vocational or technical education needs to be settled as soon as possible.

Chapter 6
Russia

Olaf Zawacki-Richter, Sergey B. Kulikov, Diana Püplichhuysen
and Daria Khanolainen

Introduction

Distance Education in the present Russian Federation and former Soviet Union has a long tradition that prevails down to this present day. This tradition causes a distinction between the Russian and international standards of distance education. In Russia, so called "distance learning" is not a term for a special mode of study at the university. It is the complex of new information and communication technologies (cf. e-learning, blended learning, flexible learning), which are applied within three main modes of study, namely, conventional on-site study at the university, regular evening courses at the university combined with self-study, and self-study combined with some hours of on-site study (Russia, 2012, §16, §17). Each mode of study at the Russian university can implement the technologies of distance learning (Russia, 2012, §17, no. 2). This chapter represents a way to understanding of the Russian forms of distance education and conditions of their coordination with the international standards.

The history of the Russian higher education system is characterized by enormous structural change, which has been procured by ideological ambitions directed towards the qualification of citizens who enjoyed only little access to higher education. Yet, at the same time it leads to problems regarding the quality of educational opportunities within distance education. Today, universities invest in the development of

O. Zawacki-Richter
Carl Von Ossietzky University of Oldenburg, Oldenburg, Germany

S. B. Kulikov (✉)
Tomsk State Pedagogical University, Tomsk, Russian Federation
e-mail: kulikovsb@tspu.edu.ru

D. Püplichhuysen
University of Münster, Institute of Economic Education, Münster, Germany

D. Khanolainen
Kazan Federal University, Kazan, Russian Federation

© The Author(s) 2019
O. Zawacki-Richter and A. Qayyum (eds.), *Open and Distance Education in Asia,
Africa and the Middle East*, SpringerBriefs in Open and Distance Education,
https://doi.org/10.1007/978-981-13-5787-9_6

"modern" online distance education, allowing for flexible study, independent of time and place. Half of the total quantity of approximately 5.2 million enrolled students in higher education is registered in distance education programs. This indicates the existence of a well-established system for distance education, of which only little is known in Western literature (see Zawacki-Richter et al., 2009; Zawacki-Richter & Kourotchkina, 2012).

Within international distance education studies, Russia remains uncharted territory. This chapter aims at shedding light on the Russian higher education system in general and distance education in Russia in particular. The first part deals with the historical development of distance education in Russia. The second part then explores the Russian higher education system, focusing on its particular structures, including the different forms of higher education institutions and modes of study. The third part demonstrates the changes in quantity of students involved in distance education at Russian universities with reference to current statistics.

Brief History of Distance Education in Russia

This part represents stages of development of adult education that lead to forming the distance education in the Russian Federation and former Soviet Union.

Adult Education in the Imperial Russia

Adult education in Russia began between the 40s and 60s of the 19th century with the foundation of "Literacy Committees" and with the development of Sunday-schools as well as the Zemstvo schools for adults in rural areas around 1860. According to the Soviet Encyclopaedia (1967–1978) approximately 27,500 Zemstvo schools had been established in Russia by 1911. This type of education was not a part of higher education. A main aim of Sunday-schools and the Zemstvo schools was the overcoming the general illiteracy. Similar to the development of the so-called correspondence schools for instruction by letter in Germany (e.g. established by Gustav Langenscheidt, cf. Zawacki-Richter, 2011), it were private institutions that predominantly initiated the development of the first print-based distance classes in Russia throughout the 2nd half of the 19th century (e.g. by the Society for the Advancement of Technical Sciences and the Society of Community Colleges). Many evening schools ("evening education") were founded around the same time as well (Rosen, Gardner, & Keppel, 1965, p. 3).

In general, adult education in the Imperial Russia served as the substitution of elementary school, helping to solve the problem of illiteracy. Higher education was an elite institution, which was not easily available for the general population (Khanin, 2008).

Russian Education in the Soviet Period

During the Soviet period, overcoming aftermaths of World War I and Civil War, and the development of industries caused involvement of the general population in educational institutions. It became the ground for the formation of specific features of distance education in Russia. The correspondence and evening schools were incorporated into the public educational system and expanded nationwide. Shortly after the October Revolution, the Communist Party demanded in its manifesto from 1919 the financial support from the government to promote the "self-education and self-development" of workers and peasants, following the ideological ambitions to elevate the educational standards of the proletariat. Three years later in 1922, a government committee for the advancement of self-education was established, which was also responsible for organizing a nationwide correspondence education system.

Various educational institutions for self-education were established thereafter, including the "Labour Faculty" (*rabochiy fakul'tet*, abbreviated *Rabfak*). Labour Faculties were not part of the higher education. These faculties were the institutions, in which workers and peasants ages 16 and up were prepared for higher education studies (Rosen et al., 1965).

Labour Faculties took the place of intermediaries between elementary schools and universities. These education opportunities can be regarded as a preliminary stage of distance education. During the academic year of 1925/26, 40% of all freshmen were graduates from Rabfaks (Soviet Encyclopaedia, 1967–1978). However, with the development of the general education system during the 1930s the Rabfaks were quickly dissolved (cf. Egorov, Vendrovsky, & Nikandrov, 2000).

In 1924, several broadcast universities for workers and peasants were established. These universities were not the real institutions of the higher education. In broadcast universities, the courses were broadcast via radio (e.g. in science of education, social sciences, engineering, radio technologies, agricultural sciences) and contained lessons ranging from 20 to 30 h. After students had listened to the lessons, they could participate in a written examination, which had to be turned in to the broadcast university for grading. However, the educational standards did not reach those of regular universities. The broadcast universities never became part of the officially accredited educational system.

The development of print-based distance education in the form of so called "correspondence education" (*zaochnoe obuchenie*) as regular part of higher education began in the 1920s:

> In August 1926, the Councils of People's Commissars made correspondence education a regular part of the higher education system. In 1927, a Central Institute for Correspondence Education was established and correspondence preparatory departments prepared young people for entering Communist universities. (Rosen et al., 1965, p. 6)

The five-year-plans for the economic development of the USSR, which had started in 1926, demanded a high quantity of qualified specialists, which the common education system failed to "produce". The correspondence study opportunities were greatly expanded. With the beginning of the 1930s, a network of correspondence education institutions and technical schools (professional schools) was established, particularly with regard to heavy industry workers and their education on-site of the factory grounds.

While, prior to 1929, distance education programs had been designed as mere self-study courses, in which the students had only little and irregular contact with teachers, the development of distance education in the following years was characterized by alternating distance—and face-to-face sessions, which can be compared to today's format of "blended learning". Nickolas de Witt, member of the Russian Research Centre at Harvard University, described the system of the different study forms as follows:

> The three basic types of instruction programs offered by Soviet higher educational establishments were: regular day, or full-time study; part-time evening; and part time extension-correspondence programs. Attempts to equate these programs with particular institutes produce a good deal of confusion. (de Witt, 1961, p. 229 et seq.)

In addition, a fourth form, the so-called "Externat" was established, in which students are not obligated to attend the university at all, instead they "merely" have to pass the final exams. In 1951, the Externat was abrogated, only to be reintroduced shortly thereafter.

Between 1940 and 1959, the quantity of part-time students enrolled in distance education courses increased by 4.5 times, while the quantity of on-campus students doubled. More than half of all students studied part time:

> In the fall of 1960, of the total 2,396,000 higher education students, 1,240,000, or 51.7 percent, were enrolled in evening or extension-correspondence programs. (de Witt, 1961, p. 231)

In 1959, the article 121 of the Russian constitution was changed and the new version emphasized the right of the Russian population to education. In order to secure that right, evening and distance education courses had to be further developed.

Against the background of the development of higher education at the Russian universities, Otto Peters, founding president of the FernUniversität in Hagen, Germany, presented a research in 1967, dealing with the "Distance Education at Higher Education Institutions in the Soviet Union". He declares, that

> [...] the high percentage of distance education students allows for the conclusion, that higher education in the Soviet Union underwent structural changes, which are unprecedented in the history of higher education. (Peters, 1967, p. 9)

Unfortunately, the enormous expansion of distance education proceeded at the expense of its quality:

> In their resolution from September, 10th, 1966, the CPSU central committee and the USSR's Council of Ministers listed the distance education system among problems, which have been solved insufficiently so far. (Peters, 1967, p. 11)

The problem of quality became one of the central issues within distance education studies in the present Russian Federation.

Post-Soviet Period

Despite the efforts to prevent distance education institutions from becoming second class schools (e.g. equal appointments to professorships etc.), the general problem of lacking quality within distance education could not be solved. The OECD report (1999) "Tertiary Education and Research in the Russian Federation" criticizes the suitability of the study material for self-study:

> There is little evidence of any kind of instructional design and, in some cases, the material provided is barely readable because of poor quality reproduction. […] Much of the material as it stands does not really enable independent study by the student. (OECD, 1999, pp. 76–79)

Due to the development of internet-based Online-education, many higher education institutions today distance themselves from traditional correspondence studies and invest in "modern" distance education. The following parts illustrate these latest developments in more detail after the Russian higher education system is described in general.

Higher Education in the Russian Federation

This part represents the argument with respect to the specifics of the forming the higher education in the Russian Federation. According to requirements of the national legislation, the educational system in the Russian Federation consists of four levels (Russia, 2012):

- Preschool education (*doschkol'noe obrazovanie*)
- General education (*obshchee obrazovanie*)
- Professional education (*professional'noe obrazovanie*)
- Continuing education (*dopolnitel'noe obrazovanie*).

Higher education falls into the branch of professional education, which consists of primary/beginning professional education, mid-level professional education, higher education and postgraduate education.

Continuous Consolidation Process

Since the dissolution of the Soviet Union in 1991, the Russian higher education system has undergone continuous reformation, of which the latest developments are all connected to the political goal of improving the quality and therefore international competitiveness of the country's universities. Political initiatives focus particularly on the consolidation of the system, which is characterized by a very high quantity of higher education institutions, many of which do not meet national and international quality standards.

According to the Russian Federal State Statistics Service (Rosstat, 2015), after the collapse of the Soviet Union the quantity of higher education institutions more than doubled in only twenty years—from 514 in the academic year 1990/91 to 1115 in 2010/11 (Rosstat, 2015). This quantity is doubled if the branches of higher education institutions in some of the 85 regions of the Russian Federation are also taken into account. In order to reduce the multiplicity of institutions, in 2012 the Russian Federal Ministry of Education and Science started a countrywide program of "efficiency monitoring" concerning higher education institutions and their branches. This exercise has been repeated annually since then, resulting in a high quantity of shut downs each year. The latest statistical survey for the academic year 2014/15 shows the quantity of higher education institutions has so far been reduced to 950. There are 548 state-owned and 402 independently operated higher education institutions in the Russian Federation (Rosstat, 2015).

Modes of Study

In Russia, there are three possible ways of studying at universities and other higher education institutions (Russia, 2012, §17, no. 2; see Table 6.1):

- conventional on-site study at the university (*ochnoe*, on-campus)
- regular evening courses at the university combined with self-study (*ochno-zaochnoe*, evening study)
- self-study combined with some hours of on-site study (*zaochnoe*, distance study per se).

From the academic year 2013/14 onwards, the former fourth type of study—the externat, i.e. pure self-study beyond sitting the final exam at the institution (Russia, 2012, §17, no. 1–2)—was officially included in the "correspondence study" group of programs (Rosstat, 2015).

Forms of Higher Education Institutions

Shutting down a considerable quantity of higher education institutions (HEIs) is seen as the only way to enlarge quality and international competitiveness of the remaining HEIs (Berghorn, 2014). Among those remaining a group of so-called "leading universities" (*veduyushchie universitety*), which are selected by means of countrywide competitions, receives special government funding. The group of "leading universities" consists of:

- the two "Autonomous Universities" Lomonosov Moscow State University (*Moskovskii Gosudarstvennyi Universitet* or *MGU*) and Saint Petersburg State University (*Sankt Peterburgskii Gosudarstvennyi Universitet* or *SPbGU*)

Table 6.1 Changes in quantity (thousands) of students since 1914 according to modes of study

Year	Total	On-campus	Distance study	Evening study	External study[a]
1914	86.5	86.5	–	–	–
1917	149.0	149.0	–	–	–
1927	114.2	114.2	–	–	–
1940/41	478.1	335.1	128.0	15.0	–
1950/51	796.7	502.6	277.1	17.0	–
1960/61	1496.7	699.2	629.9	167.6	–
1970/71	2671.7	1296.5	985.4	389.8	–
1980/81	3045.7	1685.6	959.1	401.0	–
1990/91	2824.5	1647.7	892.3	284.5	–
1995/96	2790.7	1752.6	855.8	174.8	7.5
2000/01	4741.4	2625.2	1761.8	302.2	52.2
2002/03	5947.5	3104.0	2399.9	346.0	97.6
2003/04	6455.7	3276.6	2703.7	351.3	124.1
2004/05	6884.2	3433.5	2942.5	361.8	146.4
2005/06	7064.6	3508.0	3032.0	371.2	153.4
2006/07	7309.8	3582.1	3195.9	372.3	159.6
2007/08	7461.3	3571.3	3367.9	352.9	169.2
2008/09	7513.1	3457.2	3540.7	343.7	171.5
2009/10	7418.8	3280.0	3639.2	323.6	175.9
2010/11	7049.8	3073.7	3557.2	304.7	114.1
2011/12	6490.0	2847.7	3289.7	263.4	89.2
2012/13	6073.9	2721.0	3053.3	229.6	70.0
2013/14	5646.7	2618.8	2783.9	189.2	54.7
2014/15	5209.0	2575.0	2475.5	158.5	–[b]

Rosstat (2015)

[a]Historically, this mode of study was additional to the distance education

[b]From 2013/14 onwards the "external" was integrated into the category of "distance study"

- National Research Universities
- Federal Universities
- other leading universities with a special profile, for instance Moscow State Institute of International Relations (*Moskovskii Gosudarstvennyi Institut Mezhdunarodnykh Otnoshenii (Universitet)* or *MGIMO University*).

The "Autonomous Universities" Lomonosov Moscow State University and Saint Petersburg State University, as the oldest and most prestigious classical universities of the country (Russia, 2009, §1, no. 1) received a special legal status beyond the general Law on Education in The Russian Federation of 2012 (Russia, 2012, §4, no. 8). According to the Law on the Lomonosov Moscow State University and the Saint

Petersburg State University (Russia, 2009), they are for instance permitted to establish programmes and issue degrees to their own educational standards (Russia, 2009, §4, no. 1), but with the restriction that those should not be lower than the official federal educational standards (Russia, 2009, §4, no. 2) and independently establish branches overseas (Russia, 2009, §3, no. 3). The aim of this special status is to strengthen their worldwide reputation making them the "lighthouses" of the Russian higher education system. It might seem like more autonomy but can be also interpreted as growth of the state control. The heads of the two autonomous universities are the only ones directly appointed and dismissed by the Russian President (Russia, 2009, §2, no. 5), also the two universities receive their funding directly from the Federal Budget but not by ministerial budgets as applies for the other Russian state universities (Russia, 2009, §5, no. 1).

The second group of Russian "leading universities", namely, the National Research Universities are mainly Technical Universities, which receive funding in order to build up their research activities (MON, 2015a). This is accompanied by the consolidation of the Russian Academy of Science (*Rossiiskaya Akademiya Nauk* or *RAN*), and the limitation of its autonomy by a new law issued on September 13th 2013. So far the *RAN* was exclusively responsibly for all research activities in the Russian Federation, while universities had a pure educational mandate. The law 2013 led this 300-year tradition to the end. Politics aim at reducing the size of the *RAN* and its activities while enlarging research activities of the universities, mainly of those having received the status of a National Research University (Gathmann, 2013).

The third and last group of "leading universities" are the Federal Universities, which were implemented to reach a consolidation of universities by merging the best universities of a federal district. In each Federal District one federal university was established. In addition to those universities, there is the Baltic Federal University in the exclave Kaliningrad.

Between 2010 and 2012 the "leading universities" received 90 billion Roubles of funding, and back then this equalled 2.2 billion Euros (MON, 2015b). Among "leading universities" 21 receive further funding by another government project called "Project 5-100", which aims at placing 5 Russian universities among the 100 top universities worldwide by 2020 (MON, 2015c). A very ambitious if not even unrealistic goal considering that so far only one university, the Lomonosov Moscow State University, takes a place in the top 100 of international ranking lists. And this is not even true for every ranking. In the QS-Ranking of 2014/15, the Moscow State University was ranked place 114 (QS, 2015).

Current Forms of Distance Education in Russia

The different Russian definitions of the concept of "distance education" and its various forms complicate the methodological discussion at this point, since they do not transfer to the definitions that dominate the German or Anglo-American literature. In Russia, distance education corresponds to use of new information and communication technologies (cf. e-learning, blended learning, flexible learning) during the educational process in general (Russia, 2012, §16, no. 1). It is necessary thereby to coordinate the definitions of distance education that dominate the German or Anglo-American literature with the Russian approaches. This part then describes the situation in the Russian distance education, demonstrating the changes in quantity of students involved in distance education at Russian universities with reference to current statistics.

Concepts of Distance Education

Rosen et al. (1965) use the term "Part-time education" as a broader term to describe extra occupational qualification, continuing education, and adult education as well as distance education in Russia and the USSR:

> Part-time education in the Soviet Union encompassed general education and specialized training of urban and rural youth and adults, 'without interruption of production'. The term, 'part-time education', as applied to the Soviet system may be related to educational programs in the United States known as work-study programs, continuing education, evening correspondence, and part-time study.

Nowadays the term "distance education" (*distantsionnoe obrazovanie*) in Russia is used to describe the modern version of distance education, which employs the elements of e-learning, blended learning, and flexible learning, whereas the term "correspondence education" represents the traditional Soviet system of distance education and carries a rather negative connotation. Within the Russian literature the term "distance education" is similarly discussed but conceptually isolated from the older term "correspondence education".

Russian Students enrolled in off-campus programs are—depending on their mode of study—categorized as "*ochno-zaochnoe*" [internal extrasessional] and "*zaochnoe*" [extrasessional] students (Rosstat, 2014a). Yet of those programs only some are organized in the form of modern distance education. Selected programs can be recognized by their categorization as "*distantsionnoe obrazovanie*" or "online-*obrasovanie*"), whereas the term e-learning (*elektronnoe obuchenie*) describes the technology itself (Russia, 2012, §13, no. 2).

Modern distance education is officially promoted by the Russian Government (Vlasova, 2014, p. 43), providing its implementations by various sections of the Law on Education (Russia, 2012, §16, §13, §18 etc.). The Russian Government also fosters the development and implementation of distance education and e-learning by providing project funds, for instance via the Federal Program for the Advancement of Education 2011–2015 (http://www.fcpro.ru). The aim of this program is that 85% of all teachers in schools and universities should use educational technologies effectively in their classes. Another federal program concerning the development of education for the period 2013-2020 (Russia, 2013) stresses distance education as a vital part of Lifelong Learning (*nepreryvnoe obrazovanie*), a topic of declared importance in a country suffering demographic decrease. In the federal program mentioned above lifelong learning is characterized as one of the four pillars of Russian educational politics (Russia, 2013). As stressed in the program, the future development of lifelong learning in Russia requires a "radical innovation of learning methods and technologies" (Russia, 2013). The Law on Education in the Russian Federation confirms the right of every citizen to receive lifelong learning (Russia, 2012, §10, no. 2). In this regard, HEIs play a vital role (Russia, 2013). By 2020 the percentage of 25- to 62-year-olds taking part in courses of further qualification should be raised from 26 in 2012 to 55 (Russia, 2013), while a significant part of each study should consist of self-study and Internet-based distance education (Russia, 2013).

Furthermore, various portals have been launched, providing access to over 100,000 electronic educational resources: the Russian Education Federal Portal,[1] the Federal Centre for Educational Resources[2] and the Russian General Education Portal.[3] The most current is the portal "Open Education" (*otkrytoe obrazovanie*),[4] launched by the Russian Ministry of Education and eight of the country's "leading universities" in 2015.

Statistical Fluctuations

In the last years the quantity of distance education students in Russia has decreased rapidly from 4.1 million in 2009/2010 to 2.6 million in 2014/2015. This trend corresponds with the general decline of quantity of students in Russia. In particular, student numbers fell by one third, from 7.4 million in the academic year 2009/2010 to 5.2 million in 2014/15 (see Table 6.1).

This dramatic decline can be explained by recent demographic changes in Russian society such as the decline in the birth rate, which has continued since the 1990s (Rosstat, 2014b). The quantity of 15 to 19-year-olds, i.e. potential students, fell by one third—from 9.6 million in 2009 to 6.9 million in 2014 (Rosstat, 2014a), corresponding to the likewise decline in university admissions. There is a significant demographic "hole" in the generation of potential students in the Russian Federation. This in turn causes problems for Russia's higher education institutions, even threatening the existence of some of them, since state funding has recently been made dependent upon student enrolments (Berghorn, 2014). To fill the gap, Russian higher education institutions could focus on recruiting more foreign students; so far the percentage of foreign students is very low—2.2% in 2012/13. A goal that is vigorously pursued by the Russian Government is to increase the quantity of foreign students. It is a major task and challenge for Russian higher education institutions and involved researchers.

---

[1] http://www.edu.ru/db/portal/sites/res_page.htm.
[2] http://fcior.edu.ru.
[3] http://www.school.edu.ru.
[4] www.npoed.ru.

Despite the overall decline in quantity of students in Russia, distance education remains very relevant in the Russian higher education system. Half of the 5.2 million students at Russian HEIs are enrolled as *"ochno-zaochnye"* respectively *"zaochnye"* students (Rosstat, 2014a).

The quantity of correspondence students at private institutions is higher than at state universities. In the academic year of 2014/15 only 44% of students studying at state-owned institutions but 84.3% of students studying at private institutions were enrolled in distance education courses. Looking at state-owned institutions, the percentage of students enrolled in distance education over the last five years even decreased, from 51.3% in 2009/10 while the percentage at private institutions stayed approximately the same (2009/10: 85.6%). The stronger decrease at state-owned universities could be caused by financial matters. The state funding of HEIs in Russia has recently been made dependent upon their quantity of students (Berghorn, 2014), while students enrolled in distance education are not taken into calculation.

Compared to Russia's total population of 146.2 million (in 2015), 35 out of 1000 citizens are students. In 1990/91 only 19 out of 1000 Russians studied, even though the total population amounted to 147.7 million in the same year. Still, not only quantity of students, also the share of the population enrolled in study programs has decreased over the last five years.

Russian MOOCs

After the educational achievements of the Soviet era, the Russian Federation education system lost momentum and the roughly 1000 public and private universities are therefore seeking to raise the overall quality in higher education provision. Responding to the decline in student numbers, they seek to adopt best international practice in MOOCs; engaging in inter-institutional collaborations aimed at developing high quality open online courses equal in weight to more traditional modes of study for more learners at lower costs; promoting Russian MOOCs internationally; and launching a national 'EdTech incubator' to support educational startups (Konanchuk & Volkov, 2014).

2015 saw the launch of The Open Education project (http://openedu.ru), initially involving eight of the country's leading universities, including Moscow State University, St. Petersburg State University and Moscow Institute of Physics and Technology. Ural Federal University has launched and tested the 'Examus' system to control online tests and rule out cheating or cribbing (Istomin, 2016).

The Ministry of Education and Science has drafted new regulations to allow all Russian universities to include Open Education courses in their programmes. All of the courses are developed in accordance with the federal state educational standards and the number of MOOCs currently available on this platform is 200 and continually growing.

Some characterize this new platform as the "Russian Coursera" but this is a misnomer. Open Education primarily aims to support university students, nearly all of the courses are part of higher education programmes and compulsory modules in their respective disciplines. The Open Education certificates have a unique feature for the Russian education system—they can be transferred into university credits by students studying in Russian universities. Moreover, whereas the US platform is only partly free, Russia's is entirely so, although both charge for issuing certificates (Kureev, 2015).

Two other noteworthy examples are Universarium (http://universarium.org/) and Lectorium (https://www.lektorium.tv/). Universarium mainly focuses on interdisciplinary courses for continuing professional education and retraining. Lectorium started up as a platform for sharing video-lectures and then developed into a MOOC platform which offers support to those interested in developing their own MOOCs.

The Ministry of Education and Science is encouraging more people to study online. English language MOOCs developed by the world's leading providers with the greatest potential to benefit the development of Russia are being translated into Russian, mostly by Digital October (http://www.digitaloctober.ru), official translator of Coursera's MOOCs in Russia. And there are signs that Russians are keen on seizing these opportunities. There are already more than 120,000 Russian students learning with Coursera and the number is steadily rising, even in courses that are taught in English (Konanchuk & Volkov, 2014). Russia-based users of Coursera are even more likely than their overseas counterparts to be graduates and they demonstrate significant persistence in completing their courses (Ryabchikov, 2015). A number of Russian universities already take into account, albeit informally, Coursera and edX certificates during examinations and tests and if Russian universities start to recognize Open Education, courses taken by students on Western educational platforms could also come to be accredited (Kureev, 2015).

Russia is also seeking to internationalize its MOOCs, concentrating on those subjects in which the country has traditionally been strong and have a strong worldwide reputation which makes it easier to attract international audiences—mathematics, physics, computer science, culture and art—and to this end, is creating English language versions. In this regard, the leading provider is the Higher School of Economics in Moscow, one of the preeminent economics and social sciences universities in Eastern Europe and Eurasia. It has already enrolled more than a million online students worldwide in its 56 MOOCs, 22 of which are English, which puts it in the top 10 providers of courses on Coursera (Roshchin, 2017).

MOOCs are now regarded as a greenfield development area with enormous opportunities (Konanchuk & Volkov, 2014). There are many conservative educators who are skeptical of the idea of replacing teachers with computers, fear that the use of MOOCs will lead to universities laying off staff and replacing them with high-quality online courses from the top schools, and doubtful the economics of MOOCs. For example many regional universities and colleges will need new equipment such as workstations with Web cameras and dedicated Internet access in many lecture theaters. Alexander Yevshin, director of the Ivangorod (Leningrad Oblast) campus of St. Petersburg State University of Aerospace Instrumentation, believes that in their current form, online courses are better suited to established specialists with a clear understanding of what additional knowhow they wish to acquire.

However, given that the concept and aims of online education enjoy the support of the Russian leadership, it is clearly set to come on stream fairly rapidly. Russian universities are far less independent than those in the West, so the system allows new methods technologies to be imposed 'from above' regardless of how the schools themselves may regard the interventions. The ultimate goals are to improve the quality of higher education by replacing distance learning with online courses, using the new methods and technologies to enable the programme creators produce more research resources for universities and increase quality competition in higher education by enabling students and administrators to choose their online options. As Kureev (2015) advises, the establishment of a national educational online platform and the advancement of Internet education in universities will enable Russia to strengthen its provision of higher education.

Summary and Outlook

Historically and at present, distance education has played a prominent role in the Russian educational system. Due to the different modes of delivery in distance education, a disparate picture is created which is corroborated by the different terminologies used: the traditional correspondence education on the one hand, and "the modern distance education" employing new media or e-learning, on the other hand.

As it was already shown by the OECD report (1999), the traditional print-based distance education lacked quality. Kruglov (1997) points out that the instructional design is not laid out for the specific needs of correspondence students and the study materials are often not suitable for self-study. Today, universities operating as providers of E-Learning separate themselves deliberately against this distance education of low quality. Correspondence education departments are shut down, while new online distance education programs are established.

Kruglov (1997) observes that in terms of the development of distance education as web-based e-learning, two fundamental points of view are represented in Russia, namely, the "technocratic" and the "system developing". Representatives of the first advocate a radical break with the traditional distance education and intent to newly develop the "modern" online distance learning. This point of view is widely spread in Russia which also shows in the technological orientation in the journals. In contrast, representatives of the system developing approach support a further development of distance education.

There are strong efforts by the Russian Government, and higher education institutions, for instance by the Federal Program Development of Education (Russia, 2013) and the efforts to develop Russian MOOCs, to increase the range of programs offered online as well as their quality and therefore enlarge international reputation and enrolment quantities of Russian higher education institutions.

Acknowledgements Research was partly supported by Russian Science Foundation, grant no. 15-18-10002.

References

Berghorn, G. (2014). *Zur Reform der Hochschul- und Wissenschaftslandschaft in der russischen Föderation.* Deutsches Wissenschafts- und Innovationshaus Moskau. Retrieved July 14, 2015 from http://www.dwih.ru/index.php/de/aktuell/250-zur-refor-der-hochschul-und-wissenschaftslandschaft-in-der-russischen-foerderation.html.

de Witt, N. (1961). *Education and professional employment in the U.S.S.R.* Boston: Russian Research Center, Harvard University.

Egorov, S., Vendrovsky, R., & Nikandrov, N. (2000). Russia. In K. Salimova & N. L. Dodde (Eds.), *International handbook on history of education* (pp. 355–386). Moscow: Orbita-M.

Gathmann, M. (2013). *Putins neue Unis. Russland reformiert Hochschulen und Akademien. Kritiker fürchten mehr Kontrolle durch den Staat.* In: Der Tagesspiegel vom 13.11.2013.

Istomin, D. (2016). *Examus: new level proctoring SaaS for distance examination.* Retrieved August 1, 2017. Available at https://www.slideshare.net/dmitryistomin/examus-pitch.

Khanin, G. (2008). Vysshee obrazovanie i rossiiskoe obshchestvo [The Higher Education and the Russia's Society]. *EKO [ECO Journal], 2008*(8), 75–92.

Konanchuk, D., & Volkov, A. (2014). Epoha 'greenfield' v obrazovanii. *Rektor vuza, 3,* 66–75.

Kruglov, J. G. (1997). Ergebnisse und Perspektiven des pädagogischen Fernstudiums in Rußland. *Pädagogische Rundschau, 51,* 191–200.

Kureev, A. (2015). Will MOOCs open or close Russia's universities to the world? *Russia Direct.* Retrieved August 2, 2017. Available at http://www.russia-direct.org/analysis/will-moocs-open-or-close-russias-universities-world.

MON (Ministry of Science and Higher Education of the Russian Federation, former Ministry of Education and Science of the Russian Federation). (2015a). *Universities.* Retrieved December 28, 2018 from http://5top100.ru/en/universities.

MON (Ministry of Science and Higher Education of the Russian Federation, former Ministry of Education and Science of the Russian Federation). (2015b). *World-Class Russian Education!* Retrieved December 28, 2018 from http://5top100.ru/en/documents/regulations.

MON (Ministry of Science and Higher Education of the Russian Federation, former Ministry of Education and Science of the Russian Federation). (2015c). *5-100—Russian Academic Excellence Project.* Retrieved December 28, 2018 from http://www.5top100.ru/en/about/more-about.

OECD. (1999). *Tertiary education and research in the Russian Federation.* Paris: OECD Publications.

Peters, O. (1967). *Das Fernstudium an den Hochschulen der Sowjetunion.* Hamburg: Walter Schultz Verlag KG.

QS. (2015). *QS World University Rankings 2014/15.* Retrieved February 14, 2015 from http://www.topuniversities.com/university-rankings/world-university-rankings/2014.

Rosen, S. M., Gardner, J. W., & Keppel, F. (1965). *Part-time education in the USSR.* U.S. Department of Health Education and Welfare, Office of Education.

Roshchin, S. (2017). *1 Million Users Signed up for HSE's Online Courses on Coursera.* Retrieved August 2, 2017. Available at https://www.hse.ru/en/news/edu/206022527.html.

Rosstat. (2015). *Institutions of tertiary education,* dated 25-2-2015. Retrieved May 11, 2015 from http://www.gks.ru/free_doc/new_site/population/obraz/vp-obr1.htm.

Rosstat. (2014a). *Figures and composition of the population,* dated 24-11-2014. Retrieved April 23, 2015 from http://www.gks.ru/wps/wcm/conntect/rosstat_main/rosstat/ru/statistics/population/demography/#.

Rosstat. (2014b). *Birth rate, death rate and percental increase,* dated 22-5-14. Retrieved July 16, 2015 from http://www.gks.ru/wps/wcm/connect/rosstat_main/rosstat/ru/statistics/population/demography/#.

Russia. (2009). Law on the MGU and SPbGU. Federal'nyj zakon Rossiyskoy Federatsii ot 10 noyabrya 2009g. No. 259-F3 "O Moskovskom gosudarstvennom universitete imeni M.V. Lomonossova o Sankt-Peterburgskom gosudarstvennom universitete" (Federal Law of the Russian Federation from 10th November 2009 No. 259-F3 "On the Lomonosov Moscow State

Lomonosov University and the Saint Petersburg State University"), http://www.rg.ru/2009/11/13/universitety-dok.html.

Russia. (2012). Law on Education in the Russian Federation. Federal'nyj zakon Rossiyskoy Federatsii ot 29 dekyabr 2012 g. No. 273-F3 "Ob obrazovanii v Rossiyskoy Federatsii" (Federal Law of the Russian Federation from 29th December 2012 No. 273-F3 "On the Education in the Russian Federation"), Retrieved July 16, 2015 from http://www.rg.ru/2012/12/30/obrazovanie-dok.html.

Russia. (2013). State Programme Development of Education (Government decree to enact the State Program of the Russian Federation "Development of Education" for the Period 2013–2020, issued on 15.05.2013, No. 792-r). Retrieved December 28, 2018 from http://минобрнауки.рф/документы/3409/файл/2228/13.05.15-Госпрограмма-Развитие_образования_2013-2020.pdf.

Ryabchikov, A. P. (2015). Harakteristika rossiyskoy auditorii MOOC. *Otkrytoe I distancionnoe obrazovanie, 4*(60), 80–88.

Sovietische Enzyklopädie. (1967–1978). Große Sovietische Enzyklopädie/ Большая Советская Энциклопедия (3. Aufl.). Verlag Sovietische Enzyklopädie.

Vlasova, E. S. (2014). Elektronnoe obuchenie v sovremennom vuze. Problemy, perspektivy i opyt izpol'zovaniya. Obrasovanie sevodnya i zavtra. Universum: Vestnik Gerzenovskogo univesiteta 2/2014, pp. 43–49.

Zawacki-Richter, O., & Kourotchkina, A. (2012). The development of distance education in the Russian Federation and the former Soviet Union. *International Review of Research in Open and Distance Learning, 13*(3), 165–184.

Zawacki-Richter, O. (2011). Geschichte des Fernunterrichts - Vom brieflichen Unterricht zum gemeinsamen Lernen im Web 2.0. In S. Schön & Ebner (Hrsg.), L3T - Lehrbuch für Lernen und Lehren mit Technologien. Retrieved from http://l3t.tugraz.at/.

Zawacki-Richter, O., Bäcker, E. M., & Vogt, S. (2009). Review of distance education research (2000 to 2008)—analysis of research areas, methods, and authorship patterns. *International Review of Research in Open and Distance Learning, 10*(6), 21–50.

Chapter 7
Russia—Commentary

Galia I. Kirilova

The previous chapter on Russia gives a broad picture of distance education in Russia building on earlier research in the field. It is an updated version of the article on Russian and Soviet distance education by Zawacki-Richter and Kourotchkina (2012), and provides the historical development, analysis, theoretical evaluation and statistical data. This commentary focuses briefly on the historical aims of distance education, information technologies used, issues of access, quality, power, and openness in Russian distance education.

As the authors identify, the tradition of correspondence education can be traced to a 150-year history, up until the most recent developments in distance education in the modern Russia. The Russian and Soviet experience prior to distance education and involved transforming part-time studies and correspondence education. The aim was to improve adults' literacy, their overall education levels and to prepare people for different occupations as technological progress evolved. It is important to note that literacy rates in the Russia Federation today are not alarmingly low anymore and that the levels of complexity of occupations keeps rising.

The Russian experience of distance education reflect the field's unique nature. Distance education in the Russian Federation is both a distinct mode of instruction and a method of learning. These are characterized by the active use of information technologies. Russia has a tradition of broadcasting general knowledge materials on radio. Today the Internet plays an important role in fulfilling this function and allows education to be truly accessible. Currently, the most popular distance education platforms are Moodle (70%), BlackBoard (15%), and Openet, etc. (15%) (Kirilova, Soleimani, & Vlasova, 2017).

Accessible education implies the existence of meaningful opportunities for off-campus studies. Accessibility has another layer of meaning in Russian; providing opportunities for achieving specific educational goals by making materials and

G. I. Kirilova (✉)
Kazan Federal University, Kazan, Russia
e-mail: gikirilova@mail.ru

© The Author(s) 2019

63

O. Zawacki-Richter and A. Qayyum (eds.), *Open and Distance Education in Asia, Africa and the Middle East*, SpringerBriefs in Open and Distance Education, https://doi.org/10.1007/978-981-13-5787-9_7

instructions simple enough to be understood at specific levels of preparedness. Prospective students can achieve university requirements through attending crash courses and using other educational options provided by universities. These courses are made available to people considering applying to university. This experience of providing crash courses prepared universities to cater for different learners who aim to catch up with others pursuing the same goals as they are. It is an essential factor to keep education truly accessible.

The current quality of distance education is an issue. Educational materials are not always adapted for self-study. This is consistent with our research conducted from 2008 to 2017. In order to improve the quality of distance education it is necessary to transition towards individualized paths and interactive open sources. This can be done by moving away from the traditional forms of educational materials that do not enable learners to be in control of their own learning and towards actively interacting with others. The current trends are as follows: In 2008 80% of distance courses were simply transferred from traditional correspondent education without much adaptation. The proportion of such courses in 2012 dropped to 30% and then dropped again to 20% in 2016.

In Russia distance education has historically been controlled from above. But this is changing. Distance education was first initiated and popularized by educators from various universities (Kirilova, Grunis, & Azimi, 2017). By 2012 independent educators and university activists were responsible for 80% share of all distance education while only 20% was initiated and controlled from above. Educators were actively looking for distance education opportunities. At present, however, distance education is being reordered to become more manageable and compliant to standards with the recently introduced normative documents (Kirilova et al., 2017).

The term "openness" can be understood in three important ways in Russia. First, it implies fundamental accessibility for everyone. Second, educational materials are usually open for educators to make any changes while constantly monitoring the quality of the materials. Third, the educational space is open for development by all the participants of the educational process (Cao, Kirilova, & Grunis, 2017). This allows learners to observe and learn from other people's experiences engaged in the same educational process, as well as to showcase their own achievements and experiences. These trends in Russian context that are leading to higher accessibility and openness which are ultimately facilitating the progress towards blended learning (Kirilova, 2008).

References

Cao, Y., Kirilova, G. I., & Grunis, M. L. (2017). Cooperative research projects of master's students (education programs) in the open informational educational environment. *Eurasia Journal of Mathematics, Science and Technology Education, 13*(7) 2859–2868. http://www. ejmste.com/Cooperative-Research-Projects-of-Master-s-Students-Education-Programs-in-the-Open,75080,0,2.html.

Kirilova, G. I. (2008). Printsipy informatsionno-sredovogo podkhoda k modernizatsii profes-sional'nogo obrazovaniya. *Kazanskiy pedagogicheskiy zhurnal, 8,* 54–60. (The principles of informational-environmental approach for modernization professional educational process. *Kazan Pedagogical Journal*). https://elibrary.ru/download/elibrary_12806513_72708260.pdf (in Russian).

Kirilova, G. I., Grunis, M. L., & Azimi, S. (2017). The ratio of theory, technology and practices in pedagogical education. *The European Proceedings of Social & Behavioural Sciences, 29,* 397–405. http://www.futureacademy.org.uk/files/images/upload/IFTE2017FA047F.pdf.

Kirilova, G. I., Soleimani, N., & Vlasova, V. K. (2017). A study model of collating Russian and Ira-nian experience in the field of distance learning technologies quality. *Modern Journal of Language Teaching Methods, 7*(3)583–591. http://mjltm.org/files/cd_papers/r_32_170608001237.pdf.

Zawacki-Richter, O., & Kourotchkina, A. (2012). The development of distance education in the Russian Federation and the former Soviet Union. *International Review of Research in Open and Distributed Learning, 13*(3), 165–184.

Chapter 8
South Africa

Paul Prinsloo

Introduction

Widening access was and still is one of the foundational characteristics of distance education (Peters, 2001), increasingly optimising the affordances of technology (Altbach, Reisberg, & Rumbley, 2009; Kilfoil, 2015a). While the affordances of online distance education are not disputed, current evidence seems to suggest that there is a real danger that online distance education could increase, rather than decrease inequalities (Rohs & Ganz, 2015; World Bank, 2016). In discussing the affordances but also the limitations of educational technologies, we cannot underestimate or ignore the role of context. We are "condemned to context" (Tessmer & Richey, 1997, p. 88) and we ignore the variety of factors indigenous to a particular context at our own peril. The proposal that "[c]ontext is everything" (Jonassen, 1993, in Tessmer & Richey, 1997, p. 86) therefore provides a useful interpretive lens on this overview of the evolution of online distance education in the South African *higher education* context.

In the South African context, it is impossible to understand and assess the state (and future) of online distance higher education without due consideration of the history of education prior to the first democratic elections in 1994 and various attempts to address the continuing inter-generational legacy of apartheid (Badat, 2005; Baijnath & Butcher, 2015). As a result, South African higher education is "sandwiched between systemic contextual problems inherited from past educational policies … and a generation of limitless possibilities" inherent in increasing access to a range of emerging technologies (Bozalek & Ng'ambi, 2015, p. 3).

In the context of South African higher education, the evolution of correspondence distance education to *online* distance education is a fairly recent and emerging phenomenon. Currently distance education (at the most still off-line/correspondence) as

P. Prinsloo (✉)
University of South Africa, Pretoria, South Africa
e-mail: Prinsp@unisa.ac.za

© The Author(s) 2019
O. Zawacki-Richter and A. Qayyum (eds.), *Open and Distance Education in Asia, Africa and the Middle East*, SpringerBriefs in Open and Distance Education, https://doi.org/10.1007/978-981-13-5787-9_8

a subsystem to higher education in South Africa contributes up to 40% of headcount students and approximately 30% of full-time equivalent students (DHET, 2014b). Online distance education is, however, foreseen to expand as more and more traditional campus-based higher education institutions provide online learning opportunities (DHET, 2014b).

In order to present a national, but also critical overview of online distance education in South Africa, it is vital to map the evolution of distance education in South Africa with special reference to the historical role and mandate of the University of South Africa (Unisa). I will then discuss the re-imagining of the South African post-school system as envisioned by the "White paper for post-school education and training" (DHET, 2014a) before engaging with the "Policy for the provision of distance education in South African universities in the context of an integrated post-school system" (DHET, 2014b). I will briefly discuss the provisions and implications of these provisions for online distance education before concluding with some examples of the different nuances in online distance education provision by private and public providers.

Notes on the Research Methodology

This analysis focuses on a directed content analysis (e.g., Hsieh & Shannon, 2005) of policy and regulatory framework documents referring to (online) distance education, the websites of public and private higher education institutions and personal communication. The sampling strategy involved convenient sampling, analysing publicly available documents and websites and communicating with a number of institutional role-players (such as the South African Institute for Distance Education, SAIDE) and individuals in various higher education institutions for input (see acknowledgements). This chapter does not attempt to present a comprehensive multiple-case study analysis of the forms and nuances of online distance education provision, but rather use a selection of institutions (public and private) to illustrate key trends.

The first draft of this chapter was sent to a number of individuals for comments and verification of the analysis. Respondents' input and suggestions were incorporated and are acknowledged. Though care was taken to ensure the trustworthiness of the analysis, I acknowledge that another researcher may have emphasised different elements or chosen a different approach.

Limitations to This Study

Except for the limitations already acknowledged, it is important to note that the data were collected in the middle of 2016 to the end of 2016. I acknowledge that there may have been developments since the end of 2016. This chapter focuses predominantly on post-school distance and online provision and do not take into account distance and online provision on school level (see, for example, Niemann, 2017).

A Brief Overview of the Evolution of (Online) Distance Education in South Africa

The Early Beginnings

Distance education in South Africa is synonymous with the evolution of Unisa. Unisa is one of the mega universities in the world with a student count of close to 400,000 (Baijnath & Butcher, 2015). Unisa has evolved in three relatively distinct phases—first as an examining body (called the University of the Cape of Good Hope in 1873), followed by being a correspondence institution in 1946 with the establishment of a Division for External Studies (Boucher, 1973) and then merging with two other distance education providers in 2004 (Ngengebule, 2003).

In 1980, Technikon Southern Africa (TSA) was established as the second public distance education institution in South Africa, followed in 1981 by Vista University Distance Education Campus (VUDEC) as a unit within a contact institution, namely Vista University. In terms of *private* distance education, the first to be established was INTEC College "targeting students that required skills development, vocational training and personal growth training" (Ngengebule, 2003, p. 3). Other early private providers included Lyceum College (1917), Rapid Results College (1928), Success College (1940) and Damelin College (1948)—the latter using a range of full-time, part-time opportunities. It is worth mentioning that distance education provision at this time was guided by the Correspondence Colleges Act (1965) which only applied to private provision and created a kind of self-regulating private sub-system (Davis, Goh, Malcolm, & Uhl, n.d.). Ngengebule (2003) points to the fact that when Unisa was established as a *public* distance education provider in 1946, the move was met with fierce opposition from these private sector providers (Ngengebule, 2003).

In 2001 the National Plan for Higher Education (NPHE) was published by the Ministry of Education allaying fears "by recognising the rapidly blurring distinction between contact and distance education programme provision resulting from a significant range of media used in education delivery resulting in the continuum of educational provision ranging from *pure* correspondence to face-to-face" (Ngengebule, 2003, p. 11; emphasis added). The NPHE also recognised the "increasing number of distance education programmes [that] were being offered by face-to-face institutions—also as a result of changes in information and communications technology and the search for cost-efficiency" (Ngengebule, 2003, p. 11). Already in 2001, the NPHE warned that distance education was not the panacea for the various challenges facing post-apartheid South Africa. Also of importance is the fact that up to 2002 there was a moratorium on face-to-face institutions that prevented them from offering distance education programmes. With the moratorium lifted, all higher education providers could offer distance education on a number of conditions. Mays (2016) point to the fact that the Council of Higher Education put mechanisms in place to ensure the quality of these provisions. Davis et al. (n.d.) state that in 2001 there were 65 institutions that provided distance learning in higher education. It can safely be assumed that most (if not all) of these offerings would have been correspondence education or at the most correspondence plus a range of media and online support.

In 2004 the three public distance education providers, namely Unisa, TSA and VUDEC were merged as one, dedicated, public, comprehensive distance education provider, Unisa (Badat, 2005; Blunt, 2006; Jansen, 2004). Already in 2005 it was foreseen that "any dedicated distance institution should not attempt, in terms of provision, to meet *every* higher education need, but should concentrate on areas where there is express national, social and educational need, and where economies of scale can be achieved" (Badat, 2005, p. 194; emphasis in the original). Re-imagining distance education served the explicit cause as to provide "opportunities for social advancement for historically and socially disadvantaged social groups through equity of access, opportunity, and outcomes" (Badat, 2005, p. 194).

Re-imagining Post-school Education in South Africa

In 2014 the South African post-school education landscape consisted of 23 public universities (with two more being established in 2014); 50 public technical and vocational education and training (TVET) colleges (formerly known as further education and training [FET] colleges); public adult learning centres (soon to be absorbed into the new community colleges); and several private post-school institutions (registered private FET colleges and private higher education institutions). There were also Sector Education and Training Authorities (SETAs), a National Skills Fund (NSF) and various regulatory bodies responsible for qualifications and quality assurance in the post-school system such as the South African Qualifications Authority (SAQA) and Quality Councils (DHET, 2014a). The "White Paper for post-school education and training" (DHET, 2014a) stipulates a number of aims for the future of post-school education in South Africa, inter alia:

1. a post-school system that can assist in building a fair, equitable, non-racial, non-sexist and democratic South Africa;
2. expanded access, improved quality and increased diversity of provision;
3. a post-school education and training system that is responsive to the needs of individual citizens, employers in both public and private sectors, as well as broader societal and developmental objectives (p. xi).

One of the strategies to attain the above objectives is to "…encourage all universities to expand online and blended learning as a way *to offer niche programmes*" (DHET, 2014a, p. xvi; emphasis added). The White Paper categorises e-learning "on a continuum, ranging through categories including digitally supported, digitally dependent, Internet-supported, Internet-dependent and fully online" (2014a, p. 49).

It furthermore defines its vision for blended and online learning as follows: "The DHET will also encourage all universities to expand online and blended learning as a way to offer *niche programmes*, especially at *postgraduate level*, to those who are unable to attend full-time programmes, either due to their employment status or their geographical distance from a campus" (DHET, 2014a, p. 51; emphasis added). The role of online learning is therefore very clearly defined (and possibly limited) to the provision of *niche programmes*, especially on postgraduate level. It is important to note that state funding for distance education programmes is far less than fully residential offerings. There is also a conflation between online courses and online programmes or qualifications. The regulatory framework refers to the latter and not the former. *This raises the possibility to have a fully online course as part of a non-distance programme or qualification* (Czerniewicz, 2016). In the context of this chapter, it is therefore almost impossible to get a true reflection of the exact penetration of online distance education.

In 2014 the DHET also published the "Policy for the provision of distance education in South African universities in the context of an integrated post-school system." To understand the factors that resulted in this Policy, it is necessary to point out that there was an increasing realisation of the impact of the convergence between distance education and face-to-face modes of delivery (Glennie, 2013) owing to, but not limited to the affordances of technology, assumptions about the cost of distance and online education provision, and increasing competition. Using the notion of geolocation of the *site of learning* as main variable, Glennie (2013) points to the different possibilities in the range from campus-based education with no digital support, to campus-based with digital support, to campus-based with Internet support, to remote or distance education that is Internet-dependent to fully online and distributed.

Despite (or at least amid) the increasing convergence and blurring of the boundaries between traditional face-to-face and (online) distance education, distance education provision is still seen as "a distinct subset of provision" (DHET, 2014b, p. 6). The Policy (DHET, 2014b) recognises the fact that the post-school sector has to expand dramatically and that access to ICT is not yet ubiquitous and the costs of access not always affordable to large sections of the population. It is interesting to note that the Policy does not refer to online as an essential part of distance education provision (DHET, 2014b, p. 11), but online learning is *not* excluded (see Fig. 8.1).

The Policy does not *exclude* online delivery, but opens up the space to include a range of possibilities for the use of an "appropriate combination of different media" (DHET, 2014b, p. 11). The Preamble makes it clear that the Policy is committed not only to the "appropriate integration of ICT to enhance distance education provision in both public and private universities as well as other post-schooling institutions" but also commits the government to "ensure that every post schooling student has reasonable access to affordable connectivity" (p. 7).

Addressing the increasing convergence of, or blurring of, the boundaries between different forms of delivery and increasing access to ICT, the Policy illustrates different options of technology-enabled learning as follows (Fig. 8.1).

Figure 8.1 illustrates three of the many possibilities envisioned by the Policy (DHET, 2014b, p. 9). Position 'A' presents distance education that is digitally *sup-*

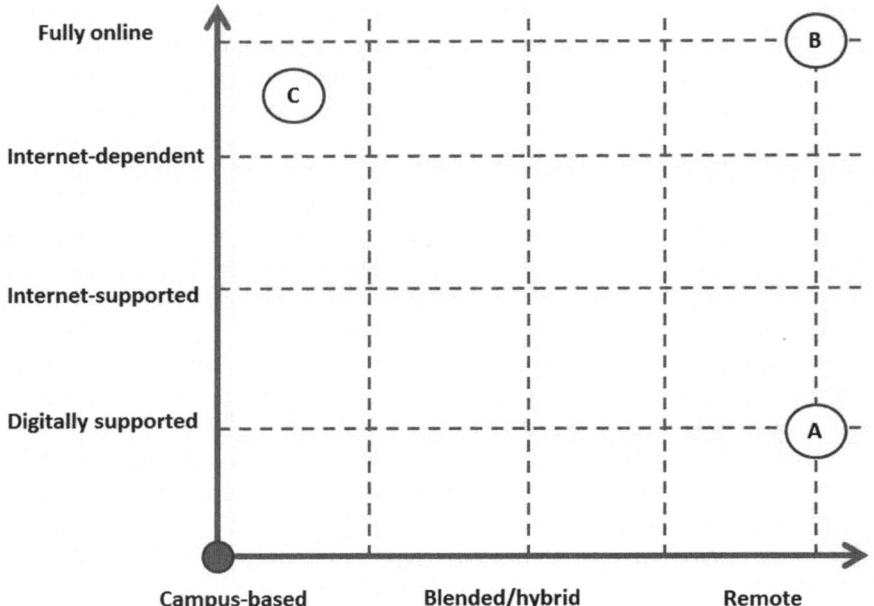

Fig. 8.1 An overview of different modes of delivery (adapted from DHET, 2014b, p. 9)

ported, while position 'B' presents a distance education scenario that is *fully online*. Position 'E' represents the possibility of a campus-based offering that is Internet-dependent with fully online elements.

In terms of the future development of these different options, the Policy (DHET, 2014b) foresees that the two main descriptions of delivery namely 'campus-based' and 'distance' will be a reality in the South African context for the "foreseeable future" (p. 9). In order to provide some more specific guidance with regard to the classification of the different nuances or possibilities as envisioned in Fig. 8.1, the Policy (DHET, 2014b) states that the notion of 'distance education' will specifically refer to a form of educational provision where "students spend 30% or less of the stated Notional Learning hours in undergraduate courses …, and 25% or less in courses" at honours and postgraduate courses that are "staff-led, campus-based structured learning activities" (p. 9).

The unique contribution and purpose of distance education as clarified above is therefore foreseen to

- Widen flexible access and meaningful, successful participation in post-school education.
- Provide "low enrolment niche programmes that have a high impact and a required by small numbers of students across the country" (DHET, 2014b, p. 12).
- Offering opportunities to students at contact institutions who need one or two outstanding modules to complete their qualifications.

• Find ways to recognise prior learning as part of widening access and create space for alternative learning pathways into post-school education.

Getting to a New Dispensation

In order to get a glimpse not only of how online distance education will continue to evolve in the South African post-school landscape, the Policy (DHET, 2014b) addresses, inter alia planning, funding, and quality assurance.

Planning

The Policy (DHET, 2014b) confirms Unisa "as the dedicated public provider of distance education in South Africa" while supporting the possibility that other institutions, (both private and public) and a variety of partnerships, may offer distance education programs that adhere to the guidelines in said Policy. In the light of concerns about quality and lack of student success in international and South African distance education, the Policy (DHET, 2014a, 2014b) emphasises the need to use student success and completions rates as measures of the efficiency and effectiveness of distance education provision.

Funding

Funding is a key steering mechanism in expanding the provision of distance education. The Policy (DHET, 2014b) commits to "exploit the potential of large-scale provision to reduce per student costs" (p. 13), while emphasising that national accreditation processes will ensure that providing institutions understand the costs (infrastructure and operational) of ensuring the efficient use of appropriate ICTs.

Traditional print-based or correspondence distance education, owing to its exploitation of scale, has always been portrayed as cheaper than traditional educational modalities. With the increasing move to online distance education, there are claims that the iron triangle of access, cost and quality is 'broken' and that online distance education can achieve high quality teaching while, at the same time, lower cost and widen participation (Daniel, Kanwar, & Uvalić-Trumbić, 2010a, 2010b). There are, however, other authors who question these claims. For example, Power and Gould-Morven (2011), suggest that the iron triangle has become "dated and fundamentally unworkable, an industrial solution in a post-industrial period" (p. 24). Hülsman (2016) questions the notion that online distance education is, necessarily, cheaper. Hülsman (2016) moots the point that distance education is cost-efficient in terms of *"cost per student"* but that distance education cannot "sustain the claim of being cost-effective in terms of *cost per graduate*" (p. 5; emphasis in the original) (also see Rumble, 2014).

The argument pertaining to the lowering of costs owing to economies of scale applies to a specific form of correspondence and industrialised distance education characterised by "the absence of responsive interaction at a distance" (Hülsman, 2016, p. 5). The inclusion of regular responsive human interaction in online distance education courses cancels the positive effects of economies of scale. Interestingly, the moment (online) distance education moves to a more interactive form of instruction and support, the purported notion of online distance education as a cheaper option becomes clear.

While the costs of online interaction are certain, Hülsman (2016) asks the critical question regarding the benefits of increased interaction specifically with regard to increased success rates. "The benefits that may accrue from STI [Student Teacher Interaction] are more uncertain than early enthusiasts would have wanted to believe. Much depends on the subject matter, educational goals, class size and instructor competence, but also on the attitude of the learners" (Hülsman, 2016, p. 18).

Considering the claims in the Policy (2014b) it is clear that the potential for lowering costs in large-scale provision can, in all probability, only be delivered *in a particular form* of distance education with very little human support and interaction. In the light of ample evidence of the under-prepared nature of distance education students in the South African higher, distance and online education contexts that necessitate (human) support and frequent feedback, the cost implications of widening access through distance education has been underestimated (Subotzky & Prinsloo, 2011).

Ensuring Quality

All qualifications (whether offered through campus-based or distance education) in the South African higher education context are accredited and quality assured by the Higher Education Quality Committee (HEQC) of the Council on Higher Education (CHE). With the widening of distance education provision, the Policy (DHET, 2014b) is clear that in cases where providers want to offer existing qualifications through distance education, that these programmes need to be re-accredited based on the minimum standards required by the National Association for Distance Education and Open Learning in South Africa (NADEOSA).

In 2014 the CHE published "Distance higher education programmes in a digital era: Good practice guide" (CHE, 2014) that aims to "assist those involved in programme design and review at institutional level as well as CHE programme evaluators involved in the accreditation process of distance education programmes, whether technology supported or not" (p. viii). The Guide (CHE, 2014) provides information and direction with regard to curriculum design, development and delivery, teaching and learning, assessment, partnerships and collaborations and the management of distance education provision in a digital era.

Some Examples Illustrating the Potential and Tensions in Moving Towards Online Distance Education

I now provide some brief examples of the emergence and evolution of online distance education in South African, private and public post-school education. In 2005, Badat stated that the number of private providers in South African higher education was still relatively small and distance education is primarily delivered by the public universities and universities of technology, and there was no significant change since then (e.g. DHET, 2014b). Online distance education is foreseen to expand as more and more traditional campus-based higher education institutions provide online distance learning opportunities (DHET, 2014b).

This section is structured as follows: I will first briefly share two examples of the state of online distance education in private higher education institutions, before discussing a selection of public higher education institutions.

Regenesys is an example of a *private* higher education provider that provides formal and short learning programmes primarily in business education (Regenesys, 2015). At Monash University all courses "are [currently] enhanced through the use of technology including having an online presence" (Cloete, 2016) and "all courses have been scheduled for a purposed blended redesign between 2015 and 2019 in order to ensure we reach an institutional objective of providing students in all programmes with at least a 25% online experience" (Cloete, 2016). Though "a number of our hybrid programmes have a fairly substantial amount of online delivery, none of these programmes currently have 30% or less (undergraduate) or 25% or less (post graduate) of their notional hours in campus based staff-led face to face contact, and thus don't meet the DHET 2014b criteria for online distance education" (Cloete, 2016).

While all courses at Stellenbosch University (SUN) have an online presence, the university currently offers no "programmes via online distance education as per definition of the DHET, 2014b" (Van der Merwe & Bosman, 2016). SUN is, however, launching its first 4-week MOOC "Teaching for change: an African philosophical approach" on 19 September (BDLive, 2016; FutureLearn, 2016). The University of the Witwatersrand (Wits) currently offers a Masters' degree in Occupational Hygiene using a combination of contact and (online) distance learning (Wits, 2016). Recently Wits announced that it will offer a "suite of online course offerings" and these will "be made available over the next three years" (BDLive, 2016). The University of Kwazulu-Natal (UKZN) currently offers "two completely online Masters programmes coordinated by the Discipline of Pharmaceutical Sciences, viz. Masters of Health Sciences and Masters of Pharmacy. The programme has students from different parts of Africa and the Middle East" (Suleman, 2016). For the last number of years *one* of the modules in the Honours degree in Information Systems was offered online (Blewitt, 2016).

The University of Cape Town (UCT) is South Africa's premier research and public, campus-based, higher education institution, currently ranked first on the African continent (US News, 2016). UCT's primary focus is foreseen to remain in the formal education arena "increasingly including fully online courses as part of traditional F2F programmes, but expanding to fully online postgraduate diplomas and degrees" (Price, 2015). Since 2014, six online distance mode qualifications have been approved with a further 14 postgraduate qualifications "either in planning, in discussion phase, in completion phase or at some approval level" (Price, 2015). UCT furthermore offers 60 short courses online (Price, 2015). UCT was the first African and South African university to develop and offer Massive Open Online Courses (MOOCs) (htxt.africa, July 2014). These MOOCs have "no entry requirements and are not for university credit" (Centre for Innovation in Teaching and Learning, 2016). Among the MOOCs offered are "Medicine and the arts: humanising healthcare", "Education for all: disability, diversity and inclusion", "What is a mind?", "Understanding clinical research: behind the statistics", and "Climate change mitigation in developing countries" (also see Walji, Deacon, Small, & Czerniewicz, 2016).

The University of Pretoria (UP) is a public campus-based higher education institution with a student enrolment in 2016 of 56,853, including 9327 distance education students. The University of Pretoria's Unit for Distance Education (UDE) within the Faculty of Education has been in existence since 2002. Since 2007 UP has adopted a blended learning approach based on a learning management system (LMS), currently Blackboard™ incorporating Blackboard Mobile, Collaborate and Analytics. Students' learning is supported by technology with more than 81.95% of the undergraduate courses having an online presence in 2014 (Department of Education Innovation, 2015). With regard to fully online courses, UP has at least six fully online Master's programme, the one in Veterinary Science running for more than a decade already. With the new hybrid model of teaching and learning adopted in 2014, there has been a major drive towards more fully online Master's programmes. The University has had small, private/professional or self-paced online courses since 2014, offered mainly through Enterprises at UP, and they were branded and launched as professional online development (POD) courses in 2015. Some will be MOOCs but others are commercial continuous professional development courses. In 2014, the Faculty of Veterinary Science launched its completely online Open Educational Resources (OER) platform for continuing professional development (Kilfoil, 2015b) (also see Zawacki-Richter, 2005).

In June 2012 North-West University (NWU) established a Unit for Open Distance Learning (UODL) on its Potchefstroom Campus. Classes are presented by facilitators or lecturers in contact mode or via interactive whiteboard. Currently 34,000 students are registered as open distance students with the majority Educational Science students and smaller numbers for Health Education and Theology students. Several other programmes from the Faculties of Arts, Economic and Management Sciences and Natural Science will be offered as distance education programmes from 2017. The UODL collaborates with the Open Learning Group (OLG) (Open Learning Group, 2016). In their collaboration with NWU, OLG is an *administrative* collaborator while the NWU is responsible for the academic programmes and especially the quality of these programmes (Combrinck, 2016).

Issues impacting on moving to fully online distance education are, amongst others, infrastructure and limited bandwidth, political and cultural factors, student access to devices, a commitment to opening content, fostering a commitment to new learning models and developing staff capacity (Baijnath & Butcher, 2015). While all Unisa courses on undergraduate and postgraduate level have an online presence with digitised learning resources and a variation and scope for interactivity, of specific interest is the 'signature courses' that are fully online (no print-based materials). These are compulsory courses offered on entry-level and students have to pass the college-specific signature module before they are allowed to graduate. Each of the six academic colleges has its own signature course, introducing students not only to the specific disciplinary knowledges in the college but, more importantly, growing students' digital literacy and engagement. "Within the context of the UNISA mass access environment (with class sizes ranging between 100 and 22,000 students), students would upon registration be divided into groups of 30. A teaching assistant would then be assigned responsibility for six groups of 30 students (a total of 180 students per teaching assistant)" (Baijnath, 2013).

While students are warned prior to registration that these modules are offered fully online, these courses make provision for learning *offline* through the provision of 'digi-bands' consisting of "a rubber wrist band with a memory stick uploaded with sophisticated software" (Baijnath, 2013) containing all the learning resources, application software, multimedia programs, and email and web browsers.

Quo Vadis?

From the preceding sections it is clear that that there are many opportunities for online distance education, but also many challenges. Among the opportunities are the immense need to use online distance education as a means to not only address the immense disparities in post-apartheid South Africa, but to respond to the huge need for flexible, affordable and quality education (DHET, 2014b). In stark contrast to the potential and need to use online distance education to increase access to quality educational opportunities, are concerns about the impact of changes in funding regimes to public providers, the lack and cost of access to digital networks, the under-preparedness of students for higher education and online distance education only equalled by these institutions' under-preparedness to provide affordable and targeted student support. It is also clear that public education cannot respond to the opportunities and challenges on their own, and that there is an urgent need for private education providers and alliances of stakeholders to become part of the solution. As South Africa is relatively late in optimising the potential of massive open online courses (MOOCs), recent developments suggest that this is changing (BDLive, 2016).

The above historical overview and examples show that *fully-fledged* online distance education in South Africa is still an emerging phenomenon, deeply influenced by the history of distance education provision, recent changes in the regulatory environment and issues surrounding access and cost of access. There is increasing evidence of selected individual course and postgraduate offerings, and a range of informal online distance education offerings as can be seen in the number of institutions that are developing MOOCs.

(In)Conclusions

This case study on the emergence and evolution of online distance education in South Africa provides ample evidence of the claim that "context is everything" (Jonassen, 1993, in Tessmer & Richey, 1997, p. 86). As the exploration of the evolution of online distance education in the South African context has shown, taking context seriously requires the slowing down of discourses and often results in the questioning of 'universal' truths regarding online distance education, such as the cost of provision (Hülsman, 2016) and the claim that online learning decreases inequalities (World Bank, 2016).

Currently, online distance education in South Africa is emerging among public, private and alliances to offer niche, short learning and specialised programmes in the formal, informal and professional development contexts. The South African case study shows that, at present, that online technologies are still, and possibly for the foreseeable future, used to *support* learning and provide resources rather than being a mainstream mode of delivery for formal public and private post-school education.

Acknowledgements I would like to acknowledge (in no particular order) the critical input and support by Jennie Glennie, Tony Mays, Fatima Rahiman and Alan Amory (all from SAIDE), Laura Czerniewicz (University of Cape Town), Wendy Kilfoil (University of Pretoria), Martin Combrinck (NWU), Craig Blewitt, Fatima Suleman and Rubby Dhunpath (all from UKZN), Antionette van der Merwe and JP Bosman (Stellenbosch University), as well as Alwyn Louw, Roy Cloete and Nicolene Murdoch (Monash University).

References

Altbach, P. G., Reisberg, L., & Rumbley, L. E. (2009). Trends in global higher education: Tracking an academic revolution. Retrieved from http://www.researchgate.net/profile/Philip_Altbach/publication/225084084_Trends_in_Global_Higher_Education_Tracking_an_Academic_Revolution/links/551ac4020cf251c35b4f5d0d.pdf.

Badat, S. (2005). South Africa: Distance higher education policies for access, social equity, quality, and social and economic responsiveness in a context of the diversity of provision. *Distance Education, 26*(2), 183–204.

Baijnath, N. (2013). Curricular innovation and digitisation at a mega university in the developing world–The UNISA "Signature Course" Project. *Journal of Learning for Development-JL4D, 1*(1). Retrieved from http://jl4d.org/index.php/ejl4d/article/view/36.

Baijnath, N., & Butcher, N. (2015). Enhancing the core business of higher education in Southern Africa through technology: Limits and possibilities. Presentation at the Vice-Chancellors Leadership Dialogue, hosted by Southern African Regional Universities Association (SARUA) in partnership with UCT and Pearson South Africa, "Global trends in technology in higher education: opportunities and challenges for African universities", Lord Charles Hotel, Somerset West, 8–9 September.

BDLive. (2016, July 19). Free online course soon a reality at Stellenbosch university. Retrieved from http://www.bdlive.co.za/national/education/2016/07/19/free-online-course-soon-a-reality-at-stellenbosch-university.

Blewitt, C. (2016). Personal communication.

Blunt, R. J. S. (2006). Challenges for the curriculum of a comprehensive university: A critical case study. *South African Journal of Higher Education, 19*(6), 1021–1032.

Boucher, M. (1973). *Spes in arduis: A history of the University of South Africa.* Pretoria: Unisa.

Bozalek, V., & Ng'ambi, D. (2015). The context of learning with technology. In W. R. Kilfoil (Ed.), *Moving beyond the hype: A contextualised view of learning with technology in higher education* (pp. 3–7). Retrieved from http://www.universitiessa.ac.za/sites/www.universitiessa.ac.za/files/Moving%20beyond%20the%20hype%20A%20contextual%20view%20of%20learning%20technology%20in%20HE_Nov%202015.pdf.

Centre for Innovation in Teaching and Learning. (2016). UCT MOOCs sign up. Retrieved from http://www.cilt.uct.ac.za/cilt/moocs-uct.

Cloete, R. (Personal communication, 26 July, 2016).

Combrinck, M. (Personal communication, 2 May, 2016).

Council on Higher Education. (2014). Distance higher education programmes in a digital era: Good practice guide. Retrieved from http://www.che.ac.za/media_and_publications/frameworks-criteria/distance-higher-education-programmes-digital-era-good.

Czerniewicz, L. (Personal communication, 7 April, 2016).

Daniel, J., Kanwar, A., & Uvalić-Trumbić, S. (2010a). Breaking higher education's iron triangle: Access, cost, and quality. *Change: The Magazine of Higher Learning, 41*(2), 30–35. https://doi.org/10.3200/chng.41.2.30-35.

Daniel, J., Kanwar, A., & Uvalić-Trumbić, S. (2010b). A tectonic shift in global higher education. *Change: The Magazine of Higher Learning, 38*(4), 16—23. https://doi.org/10.3200/CHNG.38.4.16-23.

Davis, J., Goh, A., Malcolm, L., & Uhl, K. (n.d.) Distance education in South Africa. Retrieved from http://www.saide.org.za/resources/0000000321/South%2520Africa%2520Distance%2520Education.pdf.

Department of Education Innovation. (2015). Annual report 2014. University of Pretoria.

Department of Higher Education and Training. (2014a). White paper for post-school education and training. Retrieved from http://www.che.ac.za/media_and_publications/legislation/white-paper-post-school-education-and-training.

Department of Higher Education and Training. (2014b). Policy for the provision of distance education in South African universities in the context of an integrated post-school system. Retrieved from http://www.saide.org.za/sites/default/files/37811_gon535.pdf.

FutureLearn. (2016). Teaching for change: An African philosophical approach. Retrieved from https://www.futurelearn.com/courses/african-philosophy/1.

Glennie, J. (2013). Convergence and difference between campus based and distance education: Trends in a digital age. SAIDE. Retrieved from http://www.saide.org.za/sites/default/files/Convergence_0.pptx.

Hsieh, H. F., & Shannon, S. E. (2005). Three approaches to qualitative content analysis. *Qualitative Health Research, 15*(9), 1277–1288. https://doi.org/10.1177/1049732305276687.

Hülsman, T. (2016). The impact of ICT on the costs and economics of distance education: A review of the literature. *Commonwealth of Learning.* Retrieved from https://www.col.org/resources/impact-ict-costs-and-economics-distance-education-review-literature.

htxt.africa. (2014, July 7). UCT to offer free online courses in 2015. Retrieved from http://www. htxt.co.za/2014/07/07/uct-to-offer-free-online-courses-in-2015/.

Jansen, J. (2004). Changes and continuities in South Africa's higher education system, 1994 to 2004. *Changing class: Education and social change in post-apartheid South Africa*, 293–314.

Kilfoil, W. R. (2015a). Moving beyond the hype: A contextualised view of learning with technology in higher education. Retrieved from http://www.universitiessa.ac.za/sites/www. universitiessa.ac.za/files/Moving%20beyond%20the%20hype%20A%20contextual%20view% 20of%20learning%20technology%20in%20HE_Nov%202015.pdf.

Kilfoil, W. R. (2015b). Blended learning at the University of Pretoria. Presentation at the Vice-Chancellors Leadership Dialogue, hosted by Southern African Regional Universities Association (SARUA) in partnership with UCT and Pearson South Africa, "Global trends in technology in higher education: opportunities and challenges for African universities", Lord Charles Hotel, Somerset West, 8–9 September.

Mays, T. (Personal communication, 1 April, 2016).

Ngengebule, T. (2003). An overview and analysis of policy for distance education in South African higher education: Roles identified for distance education and developments in the arena from 1948. Retrieved from http://www.saide.org.za/resources/Distance%20Education/Overview% 20of%20DE%20Policy%20in%20South%20Africa.doc.

Niemann, R. (2017). A scalable distance learning support framework for South Africa: Applying the Interaction Equivalency Theorem. *International Journal of Economics and Management, 11*(1), 89–102.

Open Learning Group. (2016). About us. Retrieved from https://www.olg.co.za/olg/index.php/ about-us.

Peters, O. (2001). *Learning and teaching in distance education*. London, UK: Routledge.

Power, M., & Gould-Morven, A. (2011). Head of gold, feet of clay: The online learning paradox. *International Review of Research in Open and Distance Learning (IRRODL), 12*(2), 20–39.

Price, M. (2015). University of Cape Town models of on-line education. Presentation at the Vice-Chancellors Leadership Dialogue, hosted by Southern African Regional Universities Association (SARUA) in partnership with UCT and Pearson South Africa, "Global trends in technology in higher education: opportunities and challenges for African universities", Lord Charles Hotel, Somerset West, 8–9 September.

Regenesys. (2015). About. Retrieved from http://regenesys.net/about/.

Rohs, M., & Ganz, M. (2015). MOOCs and the claim of education for all: A disillusion by empirical data. *The International Review of Research in Open and Distributed Learning, 16*(6), 1–19.

Rumble, G. (2014). The costs and economics of online distance education. In O. Zawacki-Richter & T. Andersen (Eds.), *Online distance education: Towards a research agenda* (pp. 197–216). Edmonton, Canada: Athabasca University Press.

Subotzky, G., & Prinsloo, P. (2011). Turning the tide: A socio-critical model and framework for improving student success in open distance learning at the University of South Africa. *Distance Education, 32*(2), 177–193.

Suleman, F. (Personal communication, 22 July, 2016).

Tessmer, M., & Richey, R. C. (1997). The role of context in learning and instructional design. *Educational Technology Research and Development, 45*(2), 85–115.

US News. (2016). University of Cape Town. Retrieved from http://www.usnews.com/education/ best-global-universities/university-of-cape-town-504187.

Van der Merwe, A., & Bosman, J. P. (Personal communication, 28 July, 2016).

Walji, S., Deacon, A., Small, J., & Czerniewicz, L. (2016). Learning through engagement: MOOCs as an emergent form of provision. *Distance Education, 37*(2), 1–16. https://doi.org/10.1080/ 01587919.2016.1184400.

Wits. (2016). Master occupational hygiene. Retrieved from http://www.mastersportal.eu/studies/ 89859/occupational-hygiene.html.

World Bank. (2016). Digital dividends. Washington: International Bank for Reconstruction and Development/The World Bank. Retrieved from http://www-wds.worldbank.org/external/default/WDSContentServer/WDSP/IB/2016/01/13/090224b08405b9fa/1_0/Rendered/PDF/World0developm0l0dividends0overview.pdf.

Zawacki-Richter, O. (2005). Online faculty support and education innovation—A case study. *European Journal of Open, Distance and E-Learning, 2005*(1), 1–12.

Chapter 9
South Africa—Commentary

Jenny Glennie and Tony Mays

Extending access has, as Prinsloo correctly points out, been the major emphasis of distance education in university education in South Africa. Elaborating on Prinsloo's theme of the importance of context, we should note that this role began in the Apartheid era. From 1959, black students were systematically denied access to all but one of the established universities. In alignment with apartheid ideology, racially segregated institutions were established, mostly in the so-called homelands. UNISA—South Africa's only distance education provider at the time—was however able to play an important role in continuing to provide access to students from all racial groups to their programmes, while all other universities were restricted to particular race and language groups.[1]

Subsequently, post-apartheid South Africa saw a huge emphasis on seeking redress to the hugely racially skewed participation rates in South Africa's university system, with UNISA and other distance education providers playing a major part in both increasing overall participation rates in university education and in increasing the proportion of black students amongst those enrolled.[2] This access was not only for those adults seeking their first possibility of tertiary study, but was also for a range of recent school-leavers who were, for a range of reasons, unable to attend a traditional face-to-face university. In 2015, this last group constitutes some 20–25% of UNISA students.

---

[1] Such students had to write exams in racially segregated venues. Graduations were also segregated.

[2] Since the dawn of democracy in 1994, enrolments of university students have doubled.

J. Glennie (✉)
South African Institute for Distance Education, Johannesburg, South Africa
e-mail: jennyg@saide.org.za

T. Mays
University of Pretoria, Pretoria, South Africa
e-mail: tony.mays@up.ac.za

© The Author(s) 2019
O. Zawacki-Richter and A. Qayyum (eds.), *Open and Distance Education in Asia, Africa and the Middle East*, SpringerBriefs in Open and Distance Education, https://doi.org/10.1007/978-981-13-5787-9_9

Unfortunately, students taking advantage of this opportunity seldom translated it into completion of a qualification. Recent figures published by South Africa's Department of Higher Education and Training (DHET), show that of a 100 distance university students who enrolled for undergraduate diplomas and degrees in 2004, just over 15 had graduated by 2014.[3] While this figure was an improvement on the 11.6% throughput rate of such students between 2000 and 2010, and is not dissimilar to some other open universities, it indicates a highly inefficient use of state resources[4] and explains Hulsman's finding, referred to in Prinsloo's article, that distance education *cannot claim* to be cost effective in terms of cost per graduate.

These distressing throughput figures not only reflect inefficient use of state resources but also lay bare the wastage of human time and talent. They call into question the quality of most distance education provision in South Africa. This concern has been a major theme of higher education policy since 1994, not only in relation to the throughput of students, assumed to result from the lack of support and feedback given to students, but in respect of the level of rote learning in many distance education programmes, particularly in teacher education. It was this concern that led to the moratorium, referred to by Prinsloo, on distance education programmes outside of the dedicated provider until 2014, and which led to the publication of the Good Practice Guide on Provision of Distance Education in a Digital Age by the Council on Higher Education. This publication also provides an interpretation of the programme accreditation criteria used in giving permission to offer distance education.

The emerging[5] digital environment provides a remarkable opportunity to improve quality: through access to a wider range of learning resources, both in terms of form (not just print) but also voices (not a single prescribed textbook which students often cannot afford); through quicker feedback on assignments; and through greater ability to interact with, support and track the progress of students. The experiment of the signature courses at UNISA referred to by Prinsloo is important for it demonstrated how such digital support resulted in a 12% improvement in course success rate.

Finally, 2015 and 2016 saw major disruption of universities in South Africa, with students protesting against the ever-rising fees and demanding free university education, and the state arguing that, in the current economic downturn, this is not affordable. This context requires South Africa to find ways of improving the cost effectiveness of university education. In this respect, distance education has two possible advantages. The first is that distance education does not require students to be in a university residence. Recent data[6] from South Africa's student financial

---

[3]This figure compares with an overall 61.4% for "contact" students over a period of 6 years. (DHET presentation to the University Capacity Development Programme Consultative Workshop, September 2016).

[4]The state subsidises around half of the cost of a university place, with student fees covering the rest.

[5]It is only in the last few years that different undersea cables reaching the shores of South Africa have enabled a rapid growth in bandwidth in major urban areas and on all university campuses. However data through 3 and 4G networks remains expensive compared to international norms.

[6]Council on Higher Education. (p 94, 2015), Vital Statistics—Public Higher Education 2013, Pretoria: CHE.

aid scheme shows that when supporting a poor student, only about 40% of the support needed relates to tuition and books, the remaining 60% is for costs relating to student residence and food. It can safely be assumed that remaining at home is considerably cheaper than moving to a residence, although the quantum is not known. The second advantage is the potential economies of scale through amortising the costs of programme design and resource development over large numbers. Here the online environment may push up the costs to make the provision more expensive than correspondence study but possibly less expensive than building and maintaining campuses. We trust that the additional support given by the online environment will reap dividends in improved success and throughput rates, but we don't yet have the data.

Meanwhile, in its quest to further extend access to universities and colleges, especially Community Colleges, our Department of Higher Education and Training has committed itself to exploring an open education system comprising a network of learning centres supported by a network of providers, and utilising wherever possible existing or newly developed open education resources.[7]

---

[7]DHET (2013), White Paper for Post-School Education and Training, Pretoria: DHET. http://www.dhet.gov.za/SiteAssets/Latest%20News/White%20paper%20for%20postschool%20education%20and%20training.pdf.

Chapter 10
South Korea

Cheolil Lim, Jihyun Lee and Hyoseon Choi

Introduction

There has been significant growth in distance education (DE) in the Republic of Korea since the Korea National Open University (KNOU) was established in 1972. Today a variety of distance education courses are offered by KNOU, seventeen cyber universities, and traditional universities. The recent government initiative to establish K-MOOCs (Korean MOOCs) is providing Korean learners with more choices in distance learning (MOE of Korea, 2015a). In particular, Korea has demonstrated successfully how a national internet infrastructure can strengthen distance education, particularly in the light of the impact of the national *informatization strategies* for distance education which were launched in 2000 (KERIS, 2013).

This chapter offers an analysis of distance education in Korea, as a model for developing countries to catch up with advanced countries in meeting the demand for higher education. First, we analyze the functions and roles of distance education in the higher and lifelong education sectors in Korea. Second, we present a brief review of the history of distance education in Korea, followed by the characteristics of distance education offered by the Korea National Open University (KNOU), cyber universities and traditional universities that offer distance and online learning. Third, we examine major legislation and policies, including the Higher Education Act, to highlight efforts that have been made to ensure the quality of distance education. Lastly, we make closing remarks about future directions and challenges of distance education in the higher and lifelong education sectors in Korea.

C. Lim (✉) · J. Lee
Seoul National University, Seoul, South Korea
e-mail: chlim@snu.ac.kr

H. Choi
Chosun University, Gwangju, South Korea

© The Author(s) 2019
O. Zawacki-Richter and A. Qayyum (eds.), *Open and Distance Education in Asia, Africa and the Middle East*, SpringerBriefs in Open and Distance Education, https://doi.org/10.1007/978-981-13-5787-9_10

Functions and Roles of Distance Education in Korea

Distance education plays a major role in Korea in making higher education widely available, particularly for the purpose of lifelong education. Since 2000, the university admission rate has reached more than 79% of high school graduates. Due to generalization of higher education, it allows people accustomed to entering of higher education through distance education. Most distance education programs focus on people who enter university after starting their careers, rather than those who have recently graduated from high school. Students who are 26 years or older make up 81% of the total student population in distance universities (MOE of Korea, 2014). More than 50% of the student population in distance and cyber universities pursue additional higher education after completing an associate's or bachelor's degree, by registering as transfer students (Jung, Park, & Jung, 2010; Hwang, Lee, & Nam, 2015). As Fig. 10.1 depicts, transfer students have increased gradually. This shows that more and more adult learners are participating in extended higher education programs at KNOU or cyber universities.

The current state of distance education in Korea has evolved from fully distance education institutions for adult learners who were not the target of traditional universities. KNOU, a public distance education institution, was established in the 1970s, and has been steadily providing opportunities for higher education to adult learners who did not have easy access to traditional universities. KNOU offers programs in traditional academic fields such as literature, law, and education, with a fee that is

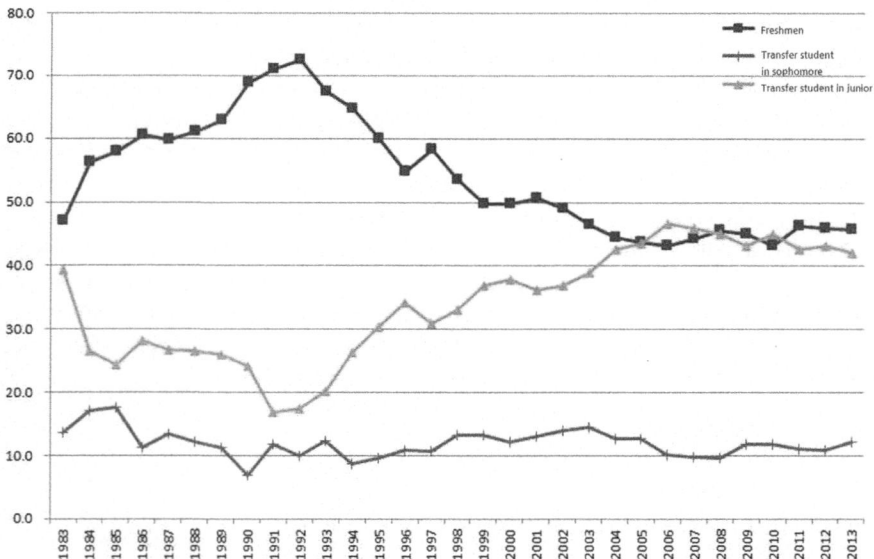

Fig. 10.1 Student popoluation in KNOU (Hwang et al., 2015)

Table 10.1 The student population of KNOU and cyber universities (Ministry of Education, Korea, 2016)

University	2010	2011	2012	2013	2014	2015	2016
Korea National Open University	272,452	268,561	254,652	245,257	227,618	214,347	184,074
Cyber Universities	93,297	103,917	106,080	109,673	109,466	111,924	114,496
Total	365,749	372,478	360,732	354,930	337,084	326,271	298,570

one third of that at cyber universities. As of 2014, KNOU had a total enrollment of more than 140,000 students (KNOU, 2014).

Cyber universities, which came into existence in 2001, have grown in number, with 17 cyber universities and two cyber colleges across the country as of 2016, with a total number of 114,496 registered students (MOE of Korea, 2016). Cyber universities offer fully online programs in sophisticated fields such as *information security management*, which reflects the characteristics and needs of an information society, and *design engineering* which mirrors the development in the field of Information and Communication Technology (ICT). Some existing traditional universities launched their own cyber universities in order to respond to the increasing demand for higher education. In the process, the number of student enrollments at KNOU has declined since 2010, while cyber universities have seen a rise in their enrollments (Table 10.1).

Since 2011, distance education practice in Korea has affected the functioning of traditional universities, with new educational methods such as massive open online courses (MOOCs) and 'flipped learning'. In addressing their social responsibilities, traditional universities have been contributing to the open courseware (OCW) movement and have developed their courses as KOCW (Korean open courseware). Such courses are supported by the Korean government for the public access. KOCW has been funded by Ministry of Education. In addition, from 2012, some universities made attempts to offer their online courses free of charge to the general public through university's funding. For example, such efforts have entered a new phase with the introduction of MOOCs by Seoul National University since 2013. K-MOOCs (Korean MOOCs)[1] were launched by Ministry of Education, Korea in 2015, with 20 free courses offered by 10 universities across the country. K-MOOCs have been financially supported by Ministry of Education and 10 universities. This distance education initiative awards students a certificate of completion at the university providing courses. This development marks the start of a new service offering in the distance education systems of traditional universities. It appears that this service will continue to expand depending on future support that may be provided by the government.

The interest of traditional universities in distance education has continued to grow with the advent of flipped learning. This teaching and learning innovation (which is

---

[1]http://www.kmooc.kr/.

called flipped classroom) is a method whereby learners are required to watch online video clips on the relevant subject matter before they attend a class (Bergmann & Sams, 2012; Han, Lim, Han, & Park, 2015). To this end, traditional universities have started making efforts to systematically publish and implement their existing courses online. Moreover, they endeavor to re-construct online courses with innovative teaching and learning model. Thus, these educational trends enable wider applications of existing theories and research findings of teaching and learning methods for distance education (Lee, Lim, & Kim, 2016). To sum up, distance education in Korea has become one of the pillars of higher education, even bringing changes to teaching and learning in traditional universities.

History of Distance Education

The distance education sector in Korea has progressed since the 1970s with increasing equity for higher education opportunities (Jung & Rha, 2006). As a result, distance education has not only increased opportunities for higher education within Korea, but is also advancing into the global arena of distance higher education (Lim, 2011; Rha, 2015; Shin, 2007). Four major development stages of distance education in Korea can be identified: *Introductory, Expansion, Rapid Growth,* and *Globalization* stages, each of which is discussed below.

Introductory stage: The first stage of distance education began in 1972 when the Korea National Open University (KNOU) was established, and continued until 1983. It was marked by *correspondence education* using postal services and *mass communication* by means of radio and television. During this period, terms such as *correspondence education* and *open education* were used within the KNOU establishment.

Expansion stage: The second stage of distance education was the period between 1984 and 1994 when distance education via radio and television was widely used. During this period, the term *distance education* emerged. The *Korea Distance Education Association* was launched in 1990, followed by the first publication of its journal in 1991, which set the stage for research into distance education.

Rapid Growth stage: The third stage of distance education was the period from 1995 (when the Internet emerged) to 2009, with explosive growth of opportunities for alternative higher education using computers and the latest digital technologies. Seventeen cyber universities were established and their accreditation, operation and evaluation were formalized. Traditional universities launched virtual campus initiatives. During this period, the base of higher education offerings through KNOU was broadened, providing equal higher education opportunities to the population. Moreover, in this period not only was a DE teaching and learning system introduced, but technical, legal and institutional systems were put in place, along with organizational changes in the higher education system. The Ministry of Education and KERIS-Korea Education and Research Information Service (2004) led the rapid growth of distance education during this period by launching the Korea Multimedia

Education Center in 1997, and assisting traditional universities to introduce virtual campuses. The Ministry of Education encouraged the establishment of cyber universities on the basis of the Lifelong Education Act and the Higher Education Act, which were enacted in 2001 and 2009 respectively.

Globalization stage: The fourth stage of distance education is the period between 2009 and today, during which distance education institutions and traditional universities, led by the government, contribute to society by offering distance education content in the form of Open Courseware (OCW) and MOOCs, thus expanding educational opportunities globally. Korean distance education, in the form of KOCW and K-MOOCs, is now available not only to the Korean general public, but to people all over the world. Such open access to content via distance education blurs the barriers between institutional education and lifelong education, by allowing high-quality educational content to be developed and distributed globally. In addition, in terms of delivery media, the period marks a sudden expansion from using PC-based internet access, which had been the norm in distance education, to mobile devices. The period also enables ubiquitous learning to take place in ever more accessible learning spaces.

The following three historical features of distance education in Korea are noteworthy. First, the introductory stage of distance education in Korea achieved in just over ten years what had taken about one hundred years to achieve regarding DE in the West. The evolutionary stages of DE (Moore & Kearsley, 1996) took place in Korea between 1972 and 1983 at full tilt, centered on radio and correspondence modes at the same time, rather than firstly mail correspondence followed by joint delivery via radio and correspondence. This is attributable mainly to the establishment of KNOU and the leading role it has played in the history of distance education.

Second, government policy and legal frameworks have been the driving force behind the expansion, rapid growth and globalization of distance education in Korea. The Ministry of Education and government-affiliated organizations took an approach to the introduction and spread of distance education that improves the people's right to higher education by expanding educational opportunities at the national level.

Third, from the early days, Korea's higher education institutions have been diversified with the establishment of various formal distance institutions, including degree-granting DE universities such as KNOU and seventeen cyber universities, with the goal of popularizing higher education. Additionally, students with a college degree have increasingly entered distance education institutions.

Major Teaching and Research Institutions for Distance Education

Korea has come to have a collection of diverse distance education institutions, thanks to rising aspirations for higher education and the demand for job retraining after employment. There are three kinds of institutions for distance education in Korea: an open university (KNOU), a cyber university, and an online course of traditional university. The Korean government has been active in promoting distance education at KNOU, cyber universities, and traditional universities through its informatization projects (KERIS, 2013). Since 2001, degree-granting distance universities are 19 institutions including KNOU, and almost all of traditional universities have provided distance courses for lifelong learning. As a result, there has been quantitative growth of distance education institutions within a short timespan.

The following sub-sections present short descriptions of KNOU, cyber universities and some traditional universities that offer distance online courses in Korea.

(1) Korea National Open University (KNOU)

The Korea National Open University (KNOU) is one of the ten mega distance education universities in the world (Daniel, 1996; Jung, 2005). Since its establishment in 1972, it has been offering undergraduate, graduate and non-degree programs. The undergraduate programs are offered by 22 departments in four colleges (humanities, social sciences, life sciences, and education), and the graduate programs are offered by 18 departments. KNOU offers more than 800 courses each year, and employs 148 full-time faculty members, 530 full-time staff, more than 3000 part-time lecturers and tutors, and 54 media production professionals.

During the 1990s, student enrollment numbers at KNOU increased every year. However, KNOU now finds itself in trouble since enrollment figures have been dropping sharply since the 2000s. Over the six years from 2009 to 2015, the number of student enrollments in undergraduate programs fell by around 40,000 (approx. 21.8%) from 183,503 to 133,385 (Hwang et al., 2015). As a result, KNOU is now focusing on trying to maintain the current number of registered students, rather than anticipating a steady drop in the future (Table 10.2).

There are three possible reasons for the declining number of student enrollments. The first reason is the high number of dropouts. In particular, many new students drop out in the first semester (Hong, Kwon, & Lee, 2004)—according to the 2008 statistics, this figure was 39.4%. KNOU has paid attention to the dropout issue and tried to solve it since its establishment. Choi, Lee, Jung, and Latchem, (2013) found that student perceptions of the value of a degree determine the possibility of dropping out. Therefore, flexible curricula and programs need to be in place to satisfy the educational needs of learners as they progress through their studies.

The second reason for falling enrollment numbers is that the educational needs of learners who may wish to enter KNOU are changing, and KNOU does not necessarily satisfy these needs (Hwang et al., 2015). In fact, even though the number of graduates has been steadily growing (with 24,000–25,000 students graduating every year), the

Table 10.2 Undergraduate enrollments at KNOU from 2009 to 2015 (Korea National Open University, 2015)

Year	2009	2010	2011	2012	2013	2014	2015
Enrollments	183,503	178,688	172,680	160,600	155,620	142,332	133,385

Table 10.3 Number of new students and enrollments at cyber universities from 2011 to 2015 (Ministry of Education, Korea, 2015b)

Year	2011	2012	2013	2014	2015
New Students	29,043	29,209	17,254	30,455	31,173
Total Enroll-ments	94,441	96,060	99,246	99,107	102,645

In accordance with the 2013 statistical guidelines for higher education, the number of junior transfers was excluded from the number of new students in 2013, hence the huge drop from 2012

number of new students has been in such decline since 2009. It leads to a net reduction in the total number of enrollments.

The third reason for falling enrollment numbers is competition from cyber universities. The enrollment numbers at cyber universities have increased (see Table 10.3), while the number of new students entering KNOU have decreased. It is clear that the reduction in the student number at KNOU is due to a move to cyber universities.

KNOU has a lower tuition fee per semester by around 300 U.S. dollars compared to other distance universities. This low tuition fee has attracted many students, and has been an important source of revenue. In fact, since the percentage of KNOU's dependence on tuition for revenue is very high (66.8%), the drop in enrollment numbers has a direct impact on the university's revenue (Ju, Nam, & Kim, 2013). Additional revenue sources are the government subsidy (25%), the university development fund (4.7%), and the university-industry cooperation fund (3.5%). Due to the drop in tuition fees, KNOU is now making efforts to increase revenue from other sources.

(2) **Cyber Universities**

Cyber universities are established by private organizations based on distance education models such as the one employed by KNOU. Anyone who graduates a high school can enter the KNOU, while cyber universities offer admissions only to qualified persons. The number of new students entering cyber universities is decided by the Ministry of Education.

Since the establishment of five cyber universities as part of government-led pilot projects in 1998, cyber universities have grown in number. There are now 19 cyber universities with the latest addition of nine more, which were accredited as higher education institutions in 2001. Undergraduate degree programs are offered by 17 cyber universities and Two cyber colleges have provided two-year college programs MOE of Korea, 2015a).

According to the 2015 White Paper on ICT in Education (MOE of Korea, 2015a), the number of students enrolled in cyber universities has been steadily increasing over the last five years. This upward trend reflects easier access to distance education with the development of Information and Communication Technology (ICT), Cyber universities offer curricula for skills that are required in the job market, including certificates that satisfy the needs of learners in terms of retraining for their job requirements.

The annual tuition fee at cyber universities is approximately 2000–3000 U.S. dollars, which is only a quarter of that at traditional universities (MOE of Korea, 2015b). Although this makes cyber universities more accessible than traditional universities, they are more dependent on enrollment numbers to continue service.

(3) **Distance Education at Campus-based Universities**

There are two dimensions of distance education offered by traditional universities in Korea. The first is the e-learning, or the so-called 'university informatization' project which almost all traditional universities in the country implement at their Centers for Teaching and Learning. Traditional universities made e-learning online courses through this project. The second is the development of open courses such as OCW or MOOCs. The following present short descriptions of e-learning and open courses in traditional universities that offer distance online courses in Korea.

The Korean government established a five-year comprehensive plan for campus informatization called 'e-Campus Vision 2007' in 2002 and launched e-Campus Support Centers at universities in ten zones. e-Campus Support Centers has helped local traditional universities to develop and share online courses. The aim was to encourage the spread of e-learning by providing subsidies to universities to develop and utilize distance educational content together. Traditional universities undertake the development and implementation of online courses as part of this informatization project (Lim, 2011). Most of them now acknowledge credits gained in online courses offered among a group of universities. In addition, traditional universities support asynchronous learning in online discussion for blended learning via Learning Management System (LMS) providing learning materials.

Many online courses developed as part of the university informatization project have become available to the public since 2009, and now are being offered as KOCW, following the global OER and OCW movements. As of 2014, 203 distance education courses developed by universities across the country were published as KOCW (MOE of Korea, 2015a). Since the launch in 2015 of the five-year comprehensive plan for campus informatization, the Ministry of Education has been promoting the improvement of teaching and learning quality for higher education through projects such as K-MOOCs and flipped learning.

Regulatory Frameworks and DE Policies

Government-led policies have played an important role in the spread of distance education at higher and distance education institutions in Korea. Moreover, the Korean government moved quickly to put the necessary laws and regulations in place, along with implementing the various policies. Legislation related to distance education in higher education falls under the 'Higher Education Act', 'Lifelong Education Act', 'Framework Act on National Infromatization', and 'Act on Development of the

Table 10.4 Legislation related to distance universities in Higher Education Act (Ministry of Education, Korea, 2015a)

	KNOU	Cyber universities
Legal Grounds	Higher Education Act Article 2 Section 5 Decree on the KNOU establishment	Higher Education Act Article 2 Section 5 Private School Act Article 3 Regulations on Cyber Universities Establishment and Operation
Basis of Implementation	Enforcement Decree of Higher Education Act	Enforcement Decree of the Higher Education Act Enforcement Decree of the Private School Act
Degrees Offered	Bachelor's Degree Master's Degree	Associate's Degree Bachelor's Degree Master's Degree

E-Learning Industry and Promotion of Utilization of E-learning (Lee, Lim, & Lim, 2009).

(1)   In addition, the basic policy framework for distance education has been updated every five years since 1996 in pursuance of the comprehensive plan for education informatization. At present, various government-led projects are underway in accordance with the fifth plan for education informatization (MOE of Korea, 2015a). To contextualize DE regulatory frameworks in Korea, the following are legislations related to the Korean distance education: Higher Education Act, Lifelong Learning Act, Framework Act on National Informatization, Act on Development of the E-learning Industry and Promotion of Utilization of E-learning.

(2)   **Higher Education Act**

Distance higher education is related to the legislations of Higher Education Act, Private School Act, Decree on the KNOU establishment, and Regulations on cyber universities Establishment and Operation.

The Higher Education Act regulates distance education services in the higher education sector. The purpose is to achieve educational equity by providing opportunities for higher education through distance education using information and communication technology. As shown in Table 10.4, distance education institutions in Korea are largely divided into KNOU and cyber universities according to classifications laid down in the Higher Education Act. Both KNOU and cyber universities are permitted offer both undergraduate and special-purpose graduate programs in pursuance of Article 2 in the Higher Education Act and Article 3 in the Private School Act. Moreover, KNOU and cyber universities are approved by Decree on the KNOU establishment and Regulations on Cyber Universities Establishment and Operation.

Table 10.5 Legislation related to Lifelong learning offering DE (Ministry of Education, Korea, 2015a)

Legal Grounds	Lifelong Education Act Article 33, Section 3 Enforcement Decree of Lifelong Education Act Article 51
Basis of Implementation	Enforcement Decree of Lifelong Education Act Enforcement Decree of Higher Education Act
Degrees Offered	Degrees equivalent to associates' or bachelors' degrees

(3) Legislation Related to Distance Lifelong Education

Some educational institutions are categorized not only as distance education institutions that are under the Higher Education Act, but also lifelong learning institutions that fall under the Lifelong Education Act. According to Article 33 of the Lifelong Education Act, these institutions are permitted to provide distance education so that everyone can receive education anywhere, anytime. However, these institutions need to be accredited and evaluated by the Ministry of Education in order to accord their degrees the same recognition as associates' or bachelors' degrees (Table 10.5).

(4) Framework Act on National Informatization

The basic plan for education informatization has been updated every five years since 1996 in line with Article 6 of the Framework Act on National Informatization. Under Article 7 of the same act, the central and municipal governments make and implement relevant action plans each year, contributing to the spread and quality improvement of distance education. According to the Framework Act on National Informatization, the Korean government has been establishing and implementing the basic plan of education informatization every five years since 1996 (MOE of Korea, 2015a). At present, policies in line with the Fifth Basic Plan for Education Informatization are being implemented. In addition, various basic plans by area and group are being established and implemented. For example, the 'Comprehensive Plan for Campus Informatization' between 2015 and 2019 aims to improve user convenience for faculty, students and staff by promoting the joint use of information resources and supporting the integration of ICT to support the strengths of each university. The vision is to achieve high quality higher education through an advanced ICT infrastructure (MOE of Korea, 2015a).

(5) Act on Development of the E-learning Industry and Promotion of Utilization of E-learning

Moreover, in accordance with Article 17, Section 2 of the Act on Development of the E-learning Industry and Promotion of Utilization of E-learning, the Ministry of Education is empowered to provide the necessary support to promote e-learning, such as the development, distribution and use of e-learning content, building models of teaching and learning, conducting e-learning consultations, and establishing an e-learning system. In addition, the Ministry of Education and heads of educational institutions are obliged by this law to work toward enhancing accessibility and convenience for socially marginalized people, while promoting e-learning. Articles 11 and 13 of the same act promote a certain level of e-learning quality with the establishment, revision of quality standards for the development of the e-learning industry.

Accreditation and Quality Assurance (QA) Systems

As a result of the significant growth in DE in Korea over the last few decades, the number of students in DE institutions has increased markedly. The quantitative expansion of DE has been a cause for growing concerns over the quality of DE programs and associated components, such as student support. The rationale behind the adoption of a QA system for DE is to ensure accountability and improve the quality of DE provision. Various stakeholders hold different views on the quality of distance education (Jung, Wong, Li, Baigatugs, & Belawati, 2011). Korean accreditation and quality assurance systems for DE acknowledge the distinctive features of DE, and accordingly apply specific QA procedures and criteria for DE, which are different from those used for traditional institutions.

There are three main systems which DE institutions in Korea implement to control the quality of distance education: accreditation, audit, and performance-based funding. Accreditation aims to ensure public responsibility for quality DE and the qualifications awarded by DE institutions. According to Jung and Latchem (2012), "[a]ccreditation is the process of external assessment and peer review that determines whether an institution (or program) qualifies for a certain status or to be recognized or certified as having met certain requirements" (p. 71). Academic audits aim to improve the quality of DE delivery. These involve both a critical self-analysis report and supporting documentation compiled by a DE institution, and an external review. The self-evaluation report is verified by means of an onsite visit by external experts who make recommendations for improvement. A subsequent monitoring process is also put in place. To stimulate competition within and between institutions, performance-based funding has been adopted, which ties public funding to the performance of an institution or a program. The outcomes of accreditation processes or academic audits are directly reflected in government funding decisions as well as the extent of administrative support provided by the government.

In Korea, all four-year universities (including KNOU) are required to conduct self-evaluations at least once every two years and submit their findings to the Korean Council for University Education (KCUE)—the only government-recognized agency allowed to accredit four-year universities. In the case of cyber universities, the Korea Education and Research Information Service (KERIS) monitors their quality programs every two years based on guidelines specified in the QA Framework for Cyber University Evaluation. These guidelines include evaluation of the following: vision, mission, values and goals; assessment and evaluation; educational resources; leadership, governance, and administration; IT infrastructure; financial resources; teaching and learning; curriculum and course development; student support; faculty and staff; and research. The QA system in distance education in Korea places particular importance on the IT infrastructure of an institution.

In the past, KERIS managed a national QA system to control the quality of e-learning content in secondary, lifelong and teacher education institutions. However, this was suspended in 2015 due to amendments made to the relevant laws.

Conclusion: Challenges and Future Directions for Distance Education in Korea

Distance education in Korea has developed rapidly and successfully to meet the demand for higher education. It has the potential to show a model for developing countries to leverage distance education for social and economic development. Since the KNOU was established in 1972, distance education has contributed to the expansion of higher education opportunities. Korean government and practitioners have made efforts to improve the equality of higher education and emphasize the innovations of distance education methods.

However, distance education in Korea is also facing unique challenges for the future development. Challenges that Korean distance education faces and related future directions can be categorized into three areas: lifelong learning, accessibility, and globalization.

First, the distance education system in Korea should pave the way for a so-called 'higher lifelong learning system' (Nam & Kim, 2013). Much of the demand for higher education which had been triggered by rapid industrialization in Korea, was met by KNOU until 2000. From 2001, ongoing demand has been actively met by private cyber universities and colleges that were established to respond to the challenges and demands of an information society. Since 2015 when traditional universities faced rapidly declining student enrollment, they have begun offering distance education opportunities to adult learners in terms of lifelong learning. In other words, as traditional universities offer distance education alongside existing full distance education institutions, the higher lifelong learning system should be ushered in by various stakeholders in the field. In that sense, it is desirable to offer a learning curriculum to meet individual learner needs.

Second, future distance education in Korea needs to be open for more learners than before. Current distance universities in Korea select their students according to the policy of the Ministry of Education which controls the number of new students (Lim, 2015). Furthermore, the pre-determined degree granting system can become barriers to the enrolment retention of distance learners. Therefore, Korean distance education should make higher education more open and more flexible to meet individual learners' needs. A potential solution could be the integration of MOOCs into distance education. The K-MOOC service first emerged in Korea in 2015. Currently limited number of K-MOOC courses provide the certificates of completion. The number of certificates granting courses are expanding, which implies the potential for diploma granting K-MOOC program. Such distance programs will play an optimistic part for higher lifelong learning in Korea.

Third, Korean distance education needs to reflect its global needs. While more and more students outside of Korea are coming to Korean campus-based universities to study and acquire diploma, limited number of foreign students are enrolling in Korean distance education programs. Current distance education of Korea does not meet global interests in Korean culture and other academic areas that Korea is leading. The developmental endeavor has mainly focused on developing educational programs for Korean learners. Korean distance education in the future needs to turn our attention to developing globalized programs for global learners. Distance education in Korea would play an important role in globalizing Korean educational services.

References

Bergmann, J., & Sams, A. (2012). *Flip your classroom: Reach every student in every class every day*. Washington, DC: ISTE & ASCD.

Choi, H., Lee, Y., Jung, I., & Latchem, C. (2013). The extent of and reasons for non re-enrollment: A case of Korea National Open University. *The International Review of Research in Open and Distance Learning, 14*(4), 1–18.

Daniel, J. S. (1996). *Mega-universities and knowledge media: Technology strategies for higher education*. Oxon: Routledge.

Han, H., Lim, C., Han, S., & Park, J. (2015). Instructional strategies for integrating online and offline modes of flipped learning in higher education. *Korean Society of Educational Technology, 31*(1), 1–38.

Hong, S. J., Kwon, J. H., & Lee, M. W. (2004). *Learner support program to improve learning retention in the first semester*. Seoul: Korea National Open University.

Hwang, J. W., Lee, K. J., & Nam, S. D. (2015). *The analysis of the determinants of enrollments* (pp. 2014–2018). Seoul: KNOU IDE policy report.

Ju, H., Nam, S., & Kim, J. (2013). *Cost analysis of education programs by teaching-learning type* (pp. 2012–2020). Seoul: KNOU IDE policy report.

Jung, I. (2005). Quality assurance survey of mega universities. In C. McIntosh & Z. Voroglu (Eds.), *Lifelong learning and distance higher education* (pp. 79–93). British Columbia: Commonwealth of Learning.

Jung, I., & Latchem, C. (Eds.). (2012). *Quality assurance and accreditation in distance education and e-learning: models, policies and research*. New York: Routledge.

Jung, Y., Park, D., & Jung, M. (2010). *Analysis of learners' characteristics in Korean distance and higher education: Comparisons between KNOU and cyber universities* (pp. 2009–2018). Seoul: KNOU IDE policy report.

Jung, I., & Rha, I. (2006). *Understanding educational technology*. Seoul: Hakjisa.

Jung, I., Wong, T. M., Li, C., Bajgaltugs, S., & Belawati, T. (2011). Quality assurance in Asian distance education: Diverse approaches and common culture. *The International Review of Research in Open and Distance Learning, 14*(4), 1–18.

Korea Education and Research Information Service (KERIS). (2013). *2013 white paper on ICT in education Korea: Summary*. KERIS PM 2013–3. Retrieved from http://english.keris.or.kr/whitepaper/WhitePaper_eng_2013.pdf.

Korea National Open University (KNOU). (2014). *KNOU education statistics*. Seoul: Korea National Open University.

Korea National Open University (KNOU). (2015). *KNOU education statistics*. Seoul: Korea National Open University.

Lee, D., Lim, C., & Lim, J. (2009). *Distance education*. Seoul: Korea National Open University Press.

Lee, J., Lim, C., & Kim, H. (2016). Development of an instructional design model for flipped learning in higher education. *Educational Technology Research and Development, 65*(2), 427–453.

Lim, C. (2011). *Understanding the applications of distance and cyber education*. Seoul: Education Science Ltd.

Lim, Y. (2015). *Restructuring types of higher education*. Sejong: Minstry of Education, Korea.

Ministry of Education, Korea. (2014). *Statistical yearbook of education*. Sejong: Ministry of Education, Korea.

Ministry of Education, Korea. (2015a). *White paper on ICT in education Korea*. Daegu: Korea Education and Research Information Service.

Ministry of Education, Korea. (2015b). Academy information. Retrieved from http://www.academyinfo.go.kr/.

Ministry of Education, Korea. (2016). *Statistical yearbook of education*. Sejong: Ministry of Education, Korea.

Ministry of Education, Korea & Korea Education and Research Information Service (KERIS). (2004). *Adpting education to the information age*. Seoul: Ministry of Education, Korea.

Moore, M. G., & Kearsley, G. (1996). *Distance education: A systems view*. Belmont, CA: Wadsworth.

Nam, S., & Kim, J. (2013). *Roles and tasks of Korea National Open University for the establishment of national smart lifelong learning systems*. Seoul: Korea National Open University.

Rha, I. (Ed.). (2015). *Global learning era: Understanding MOOCs*. Seoul: Hakjisa.

Shin, N. (2007). *Introduction to distance education*. Seoul: Seohyunsa.

Chapter 11
South Korea—Commentary

Insung Jung

The three Korean scholars' overview of distance education (DE) in South Korea illustrates the extent to which the government and, in particular, the Ministry of Education, Science, and Technology (MEST) has developed policies and procedures and initiated projects that have stimulated DE and promoted lifelong learning in collaboration with the higher education institutions.

Korea is a small country of one hundredth the size of Canada with a population of over 51 million. In the 1970s DE was first introduced by MEST in the form of the Korean National Open University (KNOU), conceived as a provider of lifelong education for the Korean people and an alternative route into higher education for those who had failed to gain entry through the highly competitive traditional system. In the 1980s, MEST not only continued to support KNOU financially but introduced the Social Education Law which allowed people to gain a Bachelor's degree through self-study without requirement for attendance at a formal institution and introduced a nation-wide educational TV channel (EBS) supplementing school education and promoting lifelong education for everyone in Korea. In the 1990s, the Ministry initiated an academic credit bank system (Usher, 2014) which allowed people to earn a Bachelor's degree by combining credits from different courses at the traditional universities, KNOU and other certified private institutions. It also authorized the establishment of wholly online 'cyber universities'. In the 2000s, the government's commitment to higher education reform, increasing access and the lifelong learning agenda led to the establishment of more cyber universities, grant funding of e-learning projects and the establishment of centers for teaching and learning development and improvement in the traditional universities. It also supported the Korea Education Research and Information Service (KERIS) in accumulating and distributing open education resources (OER) and open courseware (OCW) to the country's teachers and students, and strengthened the quality assurance system for both traditional and

I. Jung (✉)
International Christian University, Mitaka, Japan
e-mail: isjung@icu.ac.jp

© The Author(s) 2019   101
O. Zawacki-Richter and A. Qayyum (eds.), *Open and Distance Education in Asia, Africa and the Middle East*, SpringerBriefs in Open and Distance Education, https://doi.org/10.1007/978-981-13-5787-9_11

cyber universities. In 2015, the government seized on the opportunities presented by massive open online courses (MOOCs) to initiate the K-MOOC project which offered even more choices for lifelong learning.

In a country where around 80% of 4-year universities are private, operating with rigid admissions systems, these reforms and innovation in DE would not have been possible without the vision and funding provided by MEST. But the development of DE and proliferation of e-learning in higher education also owes much to the efforts of the universities and DE researchers and practitioners. For example, the Institute of Distance Education at KNOU which was founded in 1977 and the centers for teaching and learning that were established from 2003 onwards in all traditional and cyber universities as a consequence of these government interventions hired professionally trained instructional designers, e-facilitators and researchers to assist in developing, delivering and evaluating their DE courses and programs. Again as a consequence of government policy, Korea has many DE researchers and developers who have majored in instructional design and technology at both the undergraduate and graduate level, many doing so overseas. These professionals have contributed greatly to the rapid growth and quality improvement of DE and have also persuaded the government to include quality of 'instructional design effort' as an important criterion in the evaluation of all cyber and traditional universities and KNOU.

DE and the concept of lifelong learning are integral part of Korean higher education. 2016 saw the revised Lifelong Learning Act (first established in 1982) designed to remove some of the obstacles to lifelong education for workers (NILE, 2016). In that year, there were 408 higher education institutions in Korea. Of these, 189 were 4-year traditional universities with enrollment of 1,493,719, 17 were 4-year cyber universities with 97,497 students and KNOU had 123,197 students. Thus, around 14% of all 4-year university students were distance learners studying through KNOU or the cyber universities. And around 60% of the 4-year universities were offering online contents and courses for their students and exchanging their online courses with other collaborating universities (KERIS, 2016a). Again in 2016, within a year of its establishment, K-MOOC attracted and enrolled over 180,000 lifelong learners and since the introduction of OCW in 2007, over 350,000 courses had been shared and studied by adult learners following up on their personal interests and by university faculty as teaching and learning materials. These figures confirm the chapter authors' observation that DE is playing a key role in meeting the high and growing demand for higher education and lifelong learning in Korea, despite the declining population.

The chapter authors identify three challenges that DE in Korea has met: satisfying the ever-growing demand for higher levels of lifelong learning, creating a more open and flexible higher education system, and developing programs for a global audience. I would add a further serious challenge: providing such lifelong learning for the socially marginalized and less-developed parts of the country. In 2016, over 65% of KNOU students were in the capital Seoul and the larger metropolitan areas. Fewer than 1% were in the farming and fishing regions. And in the cyber universities, only 0.4% of the students were in farming and fishing communities and only 0.9% were unskilled laborers. And in the case of K-MOOC users, over 76% held a Bachelor's degree or above, and over 65% were white-collar workers or post-graduate students (KERIS, 2016b). DE in Korea has achieved a great deal but is yet to fulfill its true potential in lessening the gap between access to higher education and lifelong learning for the advantaged and disadvantaged. The government recognizes the changes in the social and industrial environment that necessitate continuous learning beyond primary and secondary education. As it seeks out new sources of growth and vies to be a world leader in innovation, it needs to ensure equity and quality education for all.

References

KERIS. (2016a). *A 2016 study on the current status of university informatization*. Seoul: Korea Education and Research Information and Service.

KERIS. (2016b). *White paper on ICT in education Korea*. Seoul: Korea Education and Research Information and Service.

NILE. (2016). Lifelong Education Act in Republic of Korea. Seoul: National Institute for Lifelong Education. Retrieved from http://hannile.cafe24.com/_upload/690720160705114953.pdf.

Usher, A. (2014). *The Korean academic credit bank: A model for credit transfer in North America?* Toronto: Higher Education Strategy Associates. Retrieved from http://higheredstrategy.com/wp-content/uploads/2014/08/Intelligence-Brief-8-Korea-Aug-17.pdf.

Chapter 12
Turkey

Yasar Kondakci, Svenja Bedenlier and Cengiz Hakan Aydin

Introduction

Bridging Asia and Europe in geography and culture, Turkey assumes a special role and unique position for South East Europe. Since its foundation in 1923, it has developed into the "18th largest economy in the world" (The World Bank, 2015, "Turkey Overview"). According to 2016 data, Turkey has a population of about 79 million with a median age of 31.0 years (Turkish Statistical Institute, 2016), which makes provision of educational services a critical public service for the country's economic and social development and realizing its transition into a knowledge society (Yilmaz, 2012). However, a digital divide between Turkey and the European Union as a direct neighbor exists (Yilmaz, 2012). Hence, providing quality education has been one of the top priorities in Turkey in its struggle to accomplish both the transition to knowledge society and its economic goals. Educational provision simultaneously constitutes a central political and societal challenge.

This chapter[1] provides an overview on the organization and practice of open and distance learning (ODL) in the context of higher education in Turkey with regard to its historical, legal, organizational and social context and role. Also addressing

---

[1]Passages of this chapter have previously been published in: Zawacki-Richter et al. (2015) or originate from earlier drafts of this article.

Y. Kondakci (✉)
Department of Educational Sciences, Middle East Technical University, Ankara, Turkey
e-mail: kyasar@metu.edu.tr

S. Bedenlier
Department of Continuing Education and Education Management, Carl von Ossietzky University, Oldenburg, Germany

C. H. Aydin
Department of Distance Education, Anadolu University, Eskişehir, Turkey

© The Author(s) 2019
O. Zawacki-Richter and A. Qayyum (eds.), *Open and Distance Education in Asia, Africa and the Middle East*, SpringerBriefs in Open and Distance Education, https://doi.org/10.1007/978-981-13-5787-9_12

current student enrolments in ODL and touching upon its major institutions, this overview closes with a brief discussion on future perspectives for ODL in Turkey.

It needs to be noted that in this chapter, the main lines of differentiation occur between open and distance education due to the fact that while open education constitutes a specified form of distance education, it follows different regulations in the Turkish case (cf. Section "Organization and Legal Framework"). ODL, on the other hand, is an umbrella term that refers to formal, informal and non-formal learning processes in which learners are separated from each others and learning resources (including instructors, materials, etc.), interaction among learners as well as learners and resources happen via telecommunication technologies.

Function and Position of ODL Within Turkish Higher Education

The increasing need for a more qualified labor force have forced Turkey to implement major educational reforms. Ensuing investments have resulted in expanded numbers and types of higher education institutions. The number of universities increased from 27 in 1982 to 53 in 1992, to 93 in 2006, and to 165 in 2011 (Günay & Günay, 2011). In 2017, there were 112 public and 67 foundation universities, i.e. with exceptions less competitive and equivalent to private universities, and five foundation vocational schools in the country (HEC, 2017). Following the significant expansion of its quantitative capacity, the higher education system now faces the challenge to also improve and maintain its overall quality (Altinsoy, 2011; Simsek, 2007).

Turkish higher education is organized in a centralized manner; the Higher Education Council (HEC) regulates all structural and functional issues (Simsek, 2007). Higher education is organized into pre-undergraduate (associate degree programs), undergraduate (bachelor degree programs), and graduate (masters degree programs and Ph.D. degree programs) levels. This three-cycle structure had already been in place before the country joined the Bologna Process in 2001. Student admission to higher education is regulated through a competitive, centralized, standardized and multi-stage examination that is annually conducted by ÖSYM, the Measurement, Selection and Placement Center, a government agency. Students have to pass with certain scores for specific study programs and universities; otherwise they need to choose a different study program at a lower-ranked university or repeat the exam.

The provision of ODL constitutes an important part of recent developments in higher education in Turkey. It is one of the main pillars in providing higher education for the masses and also constitutes the main educational practice for realizing lifelong learning; responding to in-service development needs of employed personnel in the public and private sectors who want to continue learning and update their qualifications (Selvi, 2006). Based on their analysis of Ankara University Distance Education Center, Sakarya University Distance Learning Research and Development Centre and Ahmet Yesevi University, Latchem, et al. (2009) found that: "The majority of the distance education students are aged 26–45, with around 50% in the 26–35 age group, indicating a strong demand from employees and older learners keen to improve their qualifications" (p. 11). Another core purpose of ODL is to contribute to vocational training for employed citizens, considering the large number of associate degree programs on offer. The number of four-year undergraduate programs has also increased; thus it can equally be argued that ODL also serves certification purposes. Extrapolating Latchem's et al. (2009) observation, it seems that a smaller number of ODL students seek regular higher education qualifications, while employees wanting to extend their theoretical and practical knowledge in their fields of work constitute the larger group.

Development of Turkish ODL

History of ODL goes back to early years of the Turkish Republic. In 1927, John Dewey recommended to the Ministry of National Education to adapt ODL for training teachers (Alkan, 1987). The first real implementation took place in 1956 in the corporate setting, a bank collaborated with Ankara University to initiate a correspondence study program for providing further training to its employees (Simsek, 2004). Later, several other incidents occurred in which ODL was implemented as a means to promote teaching and learning—however, these attempts give the impression of being rather tentative in nature (Aydin, 2011). In 1980, the Army in Turkey took power with the claim to end political violence between different ideological groups. The Army dissolved the Parliament and repealed the Constitution. The new military government involved in a new political and bureaucratic design with the motivation of bringing more control to state bodies. Education and specifically higher education was no exception from the new redesign of military government. After the military intervention, various reforms and paradigm shifts took place with the aim of restructuring the Turkish higher education system. Despite a new constitution and a centralized system of higher education, possibilities emerged for new types of higher education institutions.

In 1981, the existing 27 universities in Turkey could accommodate only 5.9% of the relevant age cohort (Simsek, 1999). Since ODL is usually associated with lower operational costs, this form of education is often considered as an alternative to residential higher education, particularly in developing countries (Berberoglu, 2010). Hence, one of the aims associated with its introduction was to substantially increase opportunities for higher education. During the 1980s and 1990s, ODL was also considered as a means of realizing equity by offering access to students from low socio-economic backgrounds who could not afford residential higher education programs (Selvi, 2006).

A notable milestone for ODL in Turkey was the establishment of Anadolu University's[2] (AU) Open Education Faculty in 1982. McIsaac, Murphy and Demiray (1988) state that one of the central aims of this endeavor was to "increase the availability of higher education to those for whom further education was not available before" (p. 108). Due to the number of approximately 500,000 students in the open education system in the late 1990s, AU has been considered to be a "mega-university" (Daniel, 1998, p. 29). In 2010, Istanbul University and Ataturk University established open education faculties with the prospect of sharing the load on AU—and serving as an indicator for the need to accommodate students' learning aspirations. At the turn of the twenty-first century, offering ODL alongside residential programs has become of increasing interest to Turkish universities. Recent statistics of the Higher Education Council (HEC, 2017) support this claim and show that 65 Turkish higher education institutions, including universities and vocational high schools, now offer study via distance education programs and many more provide some of their core courses (e.g. Turkish Language, English, Ataturk's Principles and History of Turkish Revolution, etc.) by means of distance education.

Organization and Legal Framework

In 1981, the first legal amendment was made to the existing higher education law and Turkish universities were given the authority to develop and deliver distance education programs. In 1982 a governmental decree authorized Anadolu University to do so. Later advancements in information and communication technologies (ICT), particularly computer networks, helped many other higher education institutions to offer ODL programs and courses. Due to ever increasing numbers of ODL offerings, several issues concerning quality and legislation have been raised. As a result, HEC differentiated the ODL implementations as Distance Education (DE) and Open Education (OE).

The basic legal document regulating DE is the "Rules and Principles of Distance Education in Higher Education Organizations" issued first in 2012 and modified in 2014 by the HEC (2014). This document does not only define DE but also regulates practices related to DE including opening programs and offering DE courses both in public and foundation universities. In this legal document, the authority of opening DE programs is given to the HEC upon the recommendation of individual higher education institutions. It also allows universities to deliver up to 30% of their total course load in the form of DE. According to this document, DE refers to an instructional model in which learners and instructors are separated geographically, and instruction is delivered mainly via synchronous ICT. In these synchronous DE programs that follow a specific course schedule, students are required to be present in front of their computer at specified times to attend online classes. Moreover, the final

---

[2]https://www.anadolu.edu.tr/en/about-anadolu/institutional/anadolu-at-a-glance (Retrieved April 10, 2016).

exam must be administered face-to-face (proctored) and constitute at least 80% of overall course grade. Additionally, because of its synchronous structure, the number of students in DE programs is limited in contrast to OE programs.

OE on the other hand, is considered as a more flexible distance-teaching model for massive audiences. The instructional strategy consists of mainly self-paced learning by using traditional educational media (textbooks, television, radio, etc.). Hence, interactivity between students and teachers is rather limited. However, synchronous or asynchronous technologies can also be used to deliver or support the instructional processes.

These two implementation models, DE and OE, also differ in terms of financial and organizational structures. In DE, the money collected from the students is an item in the overall budget of the university and all the expenses are made according to the limitations and regulations indicated in the 2014 "Rules and Principles of Distance Education in Higher Education Organizations". Meanwhile, the fees in OE go into the revolving funds of the university where there is more flexibility in expenditures. In terms of organizational structure, OE providers can have more vice-rectors than others, since organization of the OE systems requires more attention and at least one of these vice-rectors usually focuses on the OE system of the university.

In Turkey, there are four ways to enroll in an ODL undergraduate program, the *first* one being embedded into the general university entrance exam regulations and thus being subject to changes made to this centralized admission procedure over time: Before 2011 there were no quotas for OE programs (not for DE) and every student was able to enroll into their program of choice, then this was changed to the requirement of having at least 140 points in the university entrance exam that students take after graduating from secondary school. In 2017, the minimum points were raised to 180, which needed to be obtained in the second phase of the entrance exam and made students eligible for studying the 4-year undergraduate degree programs, while the two-year associate degree programs could be entered with the score from the first phase of the exam. For 2018, however, further changes to the legislation are expected, whose influence on enrolment will then need to be evaluated. *Second*, graduates of the face-to-face vocational or OE pre-undergraduate programs may choose to continue their higher education to complete their undergraduate degrees in ODL programs. In order to do so, they have to take the **external transfer exam**, organized by OSYM, and receive a score high enough to be able to register for an ODL program. Up until the beginning of 2016, students who wanted to register the OE programs (not DE) did not need to take this exam however new regulation now requires all those students to take this exam. These students can continue their education from the third year after completing required prerequisite courses (HEC, 2002). *Third*, students who are pursuing their education in a face-to-face, distance or open education program in any institution, may continue their education in an ODL program if they meet the requirements, i.e. students of an ODL program must have at least a 80 grade point average out of 100 to be able to transfer to another ODL program (HEC, 2010). *Fourth*, students who are currently pursuing an associate (pre-undergraduate) or bachelor degree may enter any OE programs without taking any exam and pursue simultaneously a second higher education degree. Similarly, those who hold a degree can also benefit from this opportunity, entitled 'second university chance'. There are a few regulations for this opportunity and the major one is about the program a student can choose to enroll: The associate degree holders or students can register for only the two year associate degree programs while bachelor degree holders or students have flexibility to choose any associate or bachelor degree program (Anadolu University 2015). In the light of above explanations, one can easily infer that opposed to the philosophy of open education, residential and distance education students are accepted according to almost the same regulations in Turkey.

Degrees gained from open, distance education and residential programs in Turkey are legally equal, thus increasing the popularity of distance programs, particularly among workers in the public sector, as diploma certification is a strong criterion for career promotion. Many distance education programs issue exactly the same certificate as the residential program offered by the particular university. In contrast, some of the degrees obtained through open education have this indicated on the certificate. However, despite equivalent legal status, open and distance learning degrees do not have equal status in practice. In most cases, a residential program diploma is preferred to an open and distance learning one, by both private and public employers (Gursoy, 2005). Even in legal graduate level, those online non-thesis degree programs are not considered as equal to face-to-face ones and graduates of these programs are not allowed to continue their studies in doctorate or PhD level (HEC, 1996).

In Turkey, accreditation and quality assurance practices are at their infancy level. Since 1980, accreditation and quality assurance practices have been scattered across different national and international bodies. During the same period of time, the HEC acted as a control mechanism for opening and executing programs in higher education, including ODE. However, the HEC had espoused a controlling role rather than giving feedback for improvement as an institution and program. In 2015, the HEC pioneered the efforts to establish an open and transparent body for accreditation and quality assurance. As a result, in 2015 the Higher Education Quality Council was established as an autonomous body for accreditation and quality assurance in Turkey. Among different roles of this body, the key one is to develop basic quality indicators for accreditation, internal and external evaluation of higher education programs (HEC, 2015), that are being applied to both residential and ODL programs. Being at the initiation stage, the Higher Education Quality Council has so far neither announced any set of quality indicators for ODL programs nor has it conducted an accreditation practice on these programs. However, individual institutions, including AU, have applied to international accreditation bodies for their programs; AU received the Pearson Assured accreditation in February 2015 for the 28 associate degree programs offered,[3] the E-xellence Quality label by the European Association for Distance Teaching Universities (EADTU) for a duration of three years followed in 2016.[4]

---

[3]https://tr.pearson.com/en/Higher-education/qualifications-development/pearson-assured.html (Last accessed Dec. 5, 2017).

[4]http://e-xcellencelabel.eadtu.eu/e-xcellence/qualified-institutions (Last accessed Dec. 5, 2017).

According to 2014 data, Turkey spends an annual 8,193 USD per tertiary education student; the country's overall spending on education being below the OECD average (OECD, 2014). The cost of ODL is quite reasonable when compared to residential programs. For instance, Anadolu University requires around US$80 for each semester-long course work, materials, and exams in its associate and bachelor degree programs. The other OE programs also ask around US$100-120 for their undergraduate programs. Although varying a bit (US$100-300), even DE providers require reasonable fees in their undergraduate programs. However, the variation in masters' level DE programs is quite high. Average fee for a semester long DE course is about US$200 but it may go up to US$1000–1200 in some institutions. Another interesting point about funding of the ODL programs is about the government's substitutions. In general, the Turkish government subsidizes nearly 95% of the tuitions in residential programs while only 5% in ODL programs.

Major ODL Teaching Institutions and Research Outlets

Anadolu University

Anadolu University's[5] OE faculty is the first and the largest institution offering OE programs in many different disciplines and is located in the city of Eskisehir. Anadolu University was established as a successor to Eskisehir Academy of Economic and Commercial Sciences in 1982 (Anadolu University, 2016a, "Anadolu at a Glance"). McIsaac, Murphy and Demiray (1988) point out that the concept of offering OE at Anadolu University was built after the already operating Open University in the United Kingdom. Recently, the OE Faculty underwent a major restructuring and now operates under the name of "open education system" (OES), which is constituted by the faculties of OE, economics, and business administration. Through the OES, Anadolu University offers nineteen four-year undergraduate degree programs in different fields of social sciences, economics and management and over 39 associate degree (pre-graduate) programs in various vocational-technical fields (Anadolu University, 2017a).

Currently, around 3 million students are enrolled in the OES at Anadolu University, herewith making it a "mega-university" (Daniel, 1998, p. 29) in that sense that it fulfills the criteria of "distance teaching, higher education, and size" (p. 29). Just taking these numbers means to acknowledge the importance and size that ODL assumes within the Turkish higher education landscape—and despite its still rather mediocre reputation regarding quality (Simsek, 2007). However, among those 3 million 1,213,352 students actively pay their fees, participate the course activities and take exams while other nearly 2 million is considered as passive students. (Anadolu University 2017b). AU is a member of the EADTU and is thus linked to the international community at the institutional level.

---

[5]https://www.anadolu.edu.tr/en/universitemiz.

Istanbul University

Like Anadolu University's OES, Istanbul University's open and distance education faculty[6] offers various programs at different levels including associate degree and undergraduate programs as well as distance undergraduate completion degrees in various fields. However, the real asset of Istanbul University's ODL faculty is related to the fact that it offers graduate programs. Undergraduate programs in OE cover history, geography, economics, management and philosophy, while DE programs cover the traditional fields of social sciences as well as some fields from hard sciences (i.e., mathematics) and media programs.

Atatürk University

The third university to offer OE is Atatürk University in Erzurum. Atatürk University's OE faculty[7] offers 20 associate degree and undergraduate degree programs in various fields of social sciences (e.g., children development, management, banking), health, media, and religious studies. Atatürk University's undergraduate programs cumulate around traditional fields of social sciences (e.g., management, sociology) as well as social work studies and public relations studies. Atatürk University explains its mission for this faculty to provide an opportunity for learning without constraints of from time and space to those people who, because of different numbers of reasons, cannot participate in any other formal higher education programs (Atatürk University, 2013). Thus, the university argues from a point of view that stresses access to higher education for a more diverse group of people.

These three major institutions are dual-mode universities. As can be seen in the table below, the number of students enrolled in an ODL program is relatively high in comparison to residential students at those universities. Even more striking is the difference when compared to the other 65 universities, which have some form or initiative of distance education; numbers of ODL students at those universities often range in the low and medium hundreds (HEC, 2017). One interpretation could be that, if the necessary infrastructure and institutionalization is in place, students actually do enroll in large numbers. Among the 65 DE providers 17 are foundation institutions (HEC, 2017). This indicates that not only public but also private institutions are interested in offering ODL. The majority of these DE providers try to focus on graduate education (masters' level degrees) due to the fact that they have more flexibility in financial issues including tuitions and fees. HEC does not allow any doctoral or PhD level ODL programs (Table 12.1).

It is also notable that Anadolu University has been internationalizing its programs by opening them to Western European countries, the Balkans (Bulgaria, Kosovo, and Macedonia, and Albania), and Azerbaijan and Northern Cyprus. It is also in preparation to offer two special bachelors program in English to reach more international students. Istanbul University and Atatürk University internationalize some of their programs by offering them to Azerbaijan.

---

[6]http://auzef.istanbul.edu.tr/.
[7]http://www.ataaof.edu.tr/#.

Table 12.1 Distribution of student numbers at Anadolu, Atatürk and Istanbul University (HEC, 2017)

University	Open education	Distance education	Residential (regular + evening classes combined)
Anadolu University	2,984,049	54	39,091
Atatürk University	204,369	4,083	67,992
Istanbul University	118,379	14,815	118,579

TOJDE and TOJET

A central means to disseminate results of research and practice in DE in Turkey is *The Turkish Online Journal of Distance Education*[8] *(TOJDE)*, which published its first volume in 2000 and has since then been published by Anadolu University (TOJDE, 2015, "Past issues"). As a peer-reviewed and open access journal, it aims at publishing articles on DE in order to inform both, theory and practice. A second Turkey-based journal is the *The Turkish Online Journal of Educational Technology (TOJET)*. It primarily focusses on educational technology and its relation to topics, such as "assessment, attitudes, beliefs, curriculum, equity, research, translating research into practice" (TOJET, no date "Submission guidelines") and is equally published as an open access journal.

Who Studies at a Distance: Enrolments in OE and DE Programs

Students who study in ODL programs are diverse. For once, they are graduates from high school who could not gain access to the residentially offered programs (Simsek, 2004). However, based on their analysis of ANKUZEM, UZEM and Ahmet Yesevi University, Latchem et al. (2009) state for programs offered at a distance that these primarily accommodate students who can be considered non-traditional. Recent figures by Anadolu University (2016b) confirm this trend: among the roughly 1.2 million active students, 44% are female, only 15% report not to work, and the largest age group is 28+ (41%). In other words, the majority of the OE students at AU are working adults or students pursuing their education in another field. These results can be regarded as an indicator of a transition from tertiary education to lifelong learning in Turkish ODL.

Hence, especially public sector workers and employees wanting to advance their careers or extend their theoretical and practical field knowledge are the primary beneficiaries of ODL. Additionally, citizens, who are not able to realize higher edu-

---

[8]http://tojde.anadolu.edu.tr/index.php?menu=33.

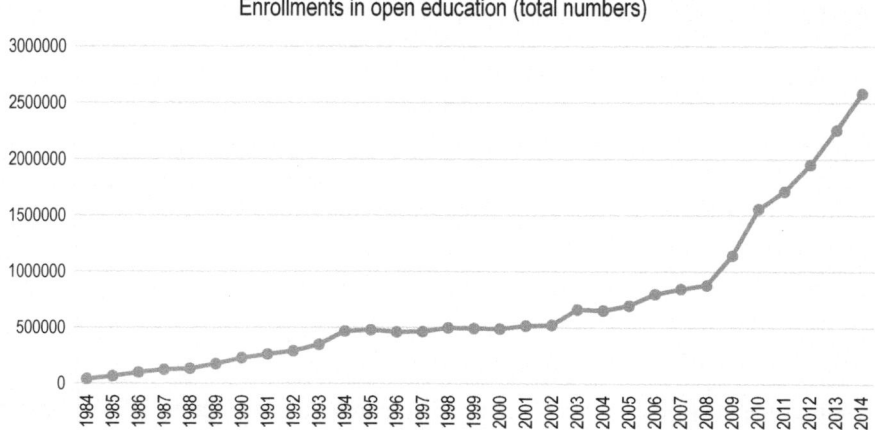

Fig. 12.1 Total student enrolment numbers in open education 1984–2014 in Turkey (own representation, data based on HEC, 2014, personal communication)

cation in residential programs due to physical handicaps, benefit extensively from ODL (Anadolu University, 2016b). In that sense, it can be argued that ODL crucially contributes to equal educational opportunity.

Figure 12.1 presents the trend in Turkish OE since its introduction. The figure shows that after the establishment of Anadolu University's OE faculty, the steady increase in student numbers also reflects the demand for OE. With the introduction of other OE faculties and multiplication of program types offered at different levels in OE faculties, enrolments experienced an even sharper incline (HEC, personal communication, December 3, 2014). While currently a total number of 91,880 students are enrolled in distance education programs (HEC, 2017), these cannot be traced back for the past years and therefore could not be included in this figure.

In addition to OE, in Turkey 65 higher education institutions offer associate, undergraduate and graduate degree DE programs. According to HEC statistics (2017), in 2017 there are 91,880 (57,521 male, 34,359 female) students enrolled in these DE programs. Out of the 65 higher education institutions, 15 offer undergraduate degree programs in engineering as well as social sciences, conferring degrees in mostly administrative sciences such as management, public administration, economics as well as media and communication sciences and engineering (computer and industrial engineering in one university). However, associate degree programs are offered by a larger number of these 65 universities in many different fields of vocational training such as health sector, public administration, tourism, banking, logistics, child development, electrical and electronics technology, ICT, etc. However, a great number of the institutions (48) offer masters' level distance education programs.

Table 12.2 reveals that ODL has a significant impact on the Turkish higher education system although these numbers might be a bit misleading due to the fact that most of the ODL student population is not active and there are some duplications (some of

Table 12.2 Higher education and ODL student population in Turkey in the 2016-2017 academic year (HEC, 2017)

	Male	Female	Total
Total Students in F2F	**2,037,573** **(54.9%)**	**1,671,470** **(45.1%)**	**3,709,043** **(52.2%)**
Associate Degree	679,173 (61.2%)	430,453 (38.8%)	1,109,626 (29.9%)
Undergraduate Degree	1,089,559 (50.7%)	1,059,607 (49.3%)	2,149,166 (58%)
Masters' Degree	268,841 (59.7%)	181,410 (40.3%)	450,251 (12.1%)
Total Students in ODL	**1,794,934** **(52.8%)**	**1,603,743** **(47.2%)**	**3,398,677** **(47.8%)**
Students in DE	**57,521** **(62.6%)**	**34,359** **(37.4%)**	**91,880** **(1.3%)**
Associate Degree	20,149 (59.4%)	13,760 (40.6%)	33,909 (36.9%)
Undergraduate Degree	11,816 (42.2%)	16,191 (57.8%)	28,007 (30.5%)
Masters' Degree	25,556 (85.3%)	4,408 (14.7%)	29,964 (32.6%)
Students in OE	**1,737,413** **(52.5%)**	**1,569,384** **(47.5%)**	**3,306,797** **(46.5)**
Associate Degree	636,449 (45.1%)	775,942 (54.9%)	1,412,391 (42.7%)
Undergraduate Degree	1,100,964 (58.1%)	793,442 (41.9%)	1,894,406 (57.3%)
Total higher education student population	**3,276,658** **(54%)**	**2,786,228** **(46%)**	**7,107,720**

the residential students are also ODL students). Still, according to 2016–2017 academic year statistics, there are 3,398,677 students in the ODL system of Turkey. Of this number, 509,591 are newly registered ones. Finally, although there is not a big difference between male and female student numbers in ODL, male student population (52.8%) is a bit more than female. However, compared to the residential (F2F) programs, this difference is smaller. On the other hand, it is interesting to see that female students pursue masters' level degrees via ODL only limitedly. Only 14.7% of the total masters' level ODL students are female and this is quite low compared to the residential ones (40.3% of students are female).

Looking Ahead: Issues and Trends

In Turkey, growing numbers in residential programs do not imply a decline in open and distance learning, as can be observed in Fig.12.1. However, there are several barriers for uptake of ODL in Turkey that are very similar to the ones indicated in the 2010 Policy Report of the International Council for Distance Education (ICDE). In this report, ICDE (2011) lists the major barriers as insufficient political goodwill, financial constraints, failure to engage allies, institutional challenges, professional deficiency, learner issues, and technological barriers. By looking at the policy declarations and programs of the government and the major political parties, it can be observed that there is no interest in ODL although it plays a crucial role in the Turkish higher education system. The HEC has adopted some policies supporting open and distance education but at the end they created conflicting results with expansion and improvement of ODL. For instance, the regulation issued in 2012 and revised in 2014 forces all the ODL providers to follow a standardized instructional strategy and does not support creative designs. During a workshop on issues of distance education in Turkey, held by Anadolu University in 2015 with the participation of major ODL providers, almost all but especially DE providers expressed their financial problems and the problematic items in the regulation. It is also observed that there is a shortage of professional organizations and meetings as well as professional programs focusing specially on ODL in Turkey. These shortages surely do not help the lack of qualified human resources (both staff and researchers). Anadolu University's graduate programs (masters' and Ph.D. level) are the only instructional programs that intend to train both researchers and practitioners.

In addition to the large young population, the growing economy pushes for an even further expansion of both residential and ODL programs. Developments in ICT suggest that not only will more programs be developed, but also that current open and distance education programs will increasingly rely on and integrate educational technology. As a result of implementing educational technology, course contents will be enriched and various delivery methods will be employed. Nevertheless, public opinion about this mode of delivery, technology literacy, technology infrastructure and the actual quality of ODL in its present form still constitute major handicaps.

So far, equality in status of degrees earned from open and distance or residential education exists only on paper. Accompanied by the traditionally held perspective towards higher education, which prioritizes traditional white-collar professions in conventional programs, DE programs as such do not receive broad interest of students. Likewise, changing employers' perception of degrees earned in open or distance education depends largely on increasing program quality.

Considering the currently available ODL programs, their quantity indicates an uncalculated expansion in ODL, which calls for a national-level strategy to become meaningful and purposeful. Along this line, a change or modification in the way DE programs are designed and delivered may be expected. This is closely related to the quality concern in DE. Factors related to academics are a major source of low quality implementation in DE (Düzakın & Yalçınkaya, 2008 as cited in Tuncer and Tanas,

2011). Academics believe that DE is more appropriate for social sciences and that it is not possible to create a conducive instructional environment (Can, 2004 as cited in Tuncer and Tanas, 2011) in other fields such as science and health.

And finally, internet use and internet access are very important indicators of broadening ODL in Turkey. According to Eurostat 2016 data (2017) Turkey is still in the low-tier countries in Europe in both household internet access (76%) and household internet use (73%). Despite the increasing trend in these two indicators, internet connectivity remains much below of the Euro Area average (internet access 85%; internet use 83%). Although these statistics do not show the distribution of these two indicators across different segments of the society, it can be suspected that disadvantaged segments of the society in Turkey have even lower access to and use of internet.

It is hoped that dealing with the problems mentioned will contribute to further expansion of ODL in Turkey. Considering the growing enrolment numbers in ODL in Turkey, it can be argued that it has the potential of serving life-long learning purposes in the country and herewith being supportive to further develop into a knowledge society. However, transforming Turkish ODL into this envisioned effective and efficient life-long learning tool as well as making it a prestigious certification mechanism relies both on transforming its present structure and function.

References

Alkan, C. (1987). *Acikögretim: Uzaktan egitim sistemlerinin karsilastirmali olarak Incelenmesi [Open Education: A comparative analysis of the distance education systems].* Ankara: Ankara University.

Altinsoy, S. (2011). A review of university facilities in Turkey. (OECD, ed.). Retrieved April 27, 2014 from http://www.oecd.org/edu/innovation-education/centreforeffectivelearningenvironmentscele/48358175.pdf.

Anadolu University (2015). Açıköğretim, İktisat ve İşletme Fakülteleri Eğitim-Öğretim ve Sınav Uygulama Esasları [Code for Education-Instruction and Exam Implementations of the Anadolu University's Open Education, Economics and Business Management Faculties]. Anadolu University Senate, 8/2, 4 October, 2015. Retrieved from http://anadolu.edu.tr/acikogretim/yonetmelikler-ve-esaslar-yonergeler/esaslar-yonergeler/anadolu-universitesi-acikogretim-iktisat-ve-isletme-fakulteleri-egitim-ogretim-ve-sinav-uygulama-esa.

Anadolu University. (2016a). Anadolu University at a Glance. Retrieved April 1, 2016 from https://www.anadolu.edu.tr/en/about-anadolu/institutional/anadolu-at-a-glance.

Anadolu University. (2016b). 2016–2017 ögretim yili güz dönemi aciköğretim sistemi ögrenci sayilari dagilimlari. Retrieved December 12, 2017 from http://argegrup.anadolu.edu.tr/upload/files/2016-2017%20AO%CC%88S%20O%CC%88G%CC%86RENCI%CC%87%20SAYILARI%20DAG%CC%86ILIMI%20gu%CC%88z.pdf.

Anadolu University. (2017a). Açıköğretim Sistemindeki Programlar. Retrieved November 10, 2017 from https://www.anadolu.edu.tr/en/open-education/programs-in-turkey.

Anadolu University. (2017b). 2017–2018 Ogretim Yılı Ekim Ogrenci Sayilari. Retrieved November 1, 2017 from https://www.anadolu.edu.tr/universitemiz/sayilarla-universitemiz/ogrenci-sayilari/2017-2018/ekim-2017.

Atatürk Universitesi Aciköğretim Fakültesi. (2013). Misyon. Retrieved January 20, 2015, from http://www.ataaof.edu.tr/hakkimizda.aspx.

Aydin, C. H. (2011). *Açık ve uzaktan öğrenme: Öğrenci adaylarının bakış açısı [Open and distance learning: Prospectus students' perspectives]*. Ankara: Pegem.

Berberoglu, B. (2010). Ekonomik performansın Anadolu Universitesi'nde uzaktan eğitim yapan fakültelerin mezun sayılarına etkisi [The effect of economic performance on the size of the distance education graduates at Anadolu University]. *Anadolu Universitesi Sosyal Bilimler Dergisi, 10*(2), 99–110.

Daniel, J. S. (1998). *Mega-universities and knowledge media: Technology strategies for higher education*. London: Kogan Page.

Eurostat. (2017). Connection to the internet and computer use. Retrieved November 15, 2017 from http://ec.europa.eu/eurostat/data/database.

Günay, D., & Günay, A. (2011). Quantitative developments in Turkish higher education since 1933. *Journal of Higher Education and Science, 1*(1), 1–22.

Gursoy, H. (2005). A critical look at distance education in Turkey. In A. A. Carr-Chellman (Ed.), *Global perspectives on e-learning: Rhetoric and reality* (pp. 115–126). Thousand Oaks, CA: Sage.

HEC. (2017). Yükseköğretim bilgi yönetim sistemi. Retrieved December 12, 2017, from https://istatistik.yok.gov.tr.

Higher Education Council. (1996). Lisansüstü eğitim ve öğretim yönetmeliği [Code for graduate education]. Resmi Gazete [Official Gazette of the Republic of Turkey], 22683, 1 July 1996. Retrieved from http://www.yok.gov.tr/web/guest/icerik/-/journal_content/56_INSTANCE_rEHF8BIsfYRx/10279/17377.

Higher Education Council (2002). Meslek Yüksekokulları ve Açıköğretim önlisans programları mezunlarının lisans öğrenimine devamları hakkındaki yönetmelik [Code for the vocational higher education schools and Open Education program graduates' completion of their undergraduate education]. Resmi Gazete [Official Gazette of the Republic of Turkey], 24676, 19 February 2002. Retrieved from http://www.yok.gov.tr/web/guest/icerik/-/journal_content/56_INSTANCE_rEHF8BIsfYRx/10279/126273.

Higher Education Council. (2010). Yükseköğretim kurumlarinda önlisans ve lisans düzeyindeki programlar arasinda geçiş, çift anadal, yan dal ile kurumlar arasi kredi transferi yapilmasi esaslarina ilişkin yönetmelik [Code for internal transfer system, pursuing major and minor degrees, and external credit transfer system]. Resmi Gazete [Official Gazette of the Republic of Turkey], 27561, 24 Nisan 2010. Retrieved from http://www.yok.gov.tr/web/guest/icerik/-/journal_content/56_INSTANCE_rEHF8BIsfYRx/10279/18082.

Higher Education Council. (2014). Yükseköğretim Kurumlarinda uzaktan öğretime iliskin usul ve esaslar. Retrieved from https://www.yok.gov.tr/documents/10279/38502/uzaktan_ogretim_esas_usul_25022014.pdf/78353e67-ac60-46d4-85b1-10a3f4cec880.

Higher Education Council. (2015). Yükseköğretim Kalite Kurulu Bilgi Notu [Higher Education Quality Council: Annotation]. Retrieved March 17, 2016, from http://www.yok.gov.tr/documents/10279/20633177/kalite_kurulu_kurulus_asamasi_bilgilendirme_notu.pdf.

International Council for Distance Education (2011). 2010 Policy Report. ICDE. Retrieved March 17, 2016 from https://issuu.com/icde/docs/icde_progress_report_june_2011_pdf.

Latchem, C., Simsek, N., Cakir Balta, Ö., Torkul, O., Cedimoglu, I. H., & Altunkopru, A. (2009). Are we there yet? A progress report from three Turkish university pioneers in distance education and e-learning. *International Review of Research in Open & Distance Learning, 10*(2).

McIsaac, M. S., Murphy, K. L., & Demiray, U. (1988). Examining distance education in Turkey. *Distance Education, 9*(1), 106–114.

OECD. (2014). Country Note: Turkey. Retrieved June 10, 2016 from https://www.oecd.org/edu/Turkey-EAG2014-Country-Note.pdf.

Selvi, K. (2006). Right of education and distance learning. *Euroasian Journal of Educational Research, 22*, 201–211.

Simsek, H. (1999). The Turkish Higher Education System in the 1990s. *Mediterranean Journal of Educational Studies, 4*(2), 133–153.

Simsek, A. (2004). Distance education—Public policy and practice in higher education: the case of Türkiye. *Brazilian Review of Open and Distance Learning, 3*.

Simsek, H. (2007). Turkey. In J. J. F. Forest & P. G. Altbach (Eds.), *International handbook of higher education* (reprinted Vol. 2, pp. 1003–1018). Dordrecht: Springer.

Tuncer, M., & Tanas, R. (2011). The evaluation of academicians' views on distance education programs (The samples of Fırat and Tunceli Universities). *Elementary Education Online, 10*(2), 776–784.

Turkish Statistical Institute. (2016). Basic statistics: Population and demography. Retrieved March 17, 2016 from http://tuik.gov.tr/UstMenu.do?metod=temelist.

The World Bank. (2015).Turkey Overview. Retrieved January 8, 2015 from http://www.worldbank. org/en/country/turkey/overview.

TOJDE. (2015). Past issues. Retrieved January 8, 2015, from http://tojde.anadolu.edu.tr/index.php? menu_v=onceki_sayilar.

TOJET. (n.d.). Submission guidelines. Retrieved June 10, 2016 from http://www.tojet.net/.

Yilmaz, Y. (2012). Transition to knowledge society in Turkey: Current state and future perspectives. *Turkish Studies, 13*(3).

Zawacki-Richter, O., Kondakci, Y., Bedenlier, S., Alturki, U., Aldraiweesh, A., & Püplychhuysen, D. (2015). The Development of Distance Education Systems in Turkey, the Russian Federation and Saudi Arabia. *European Journal of Open, Distance and E-Learning, 18*(2), 113–129.

Chapter 13
Turkey—Commentary

Soner Yildirim and Müge Adnan

Changing the face of higher education with its functions and missions revisited has made it difficult to define the 'modern campus', which may require various descriptions. Nonetheless, it is easier to see the picture through certain specific commonalities that modern campuses have (e.g. learning opportunities available anytime/anyplace, classes constructed of modular learning objects, continuous collaboration, applied research, accessible digital library) where learners are 'everybody the institution connects with teachers' in an interactive and learner-centred environment (Langenberg & Spicer, 2001, p.11). New possibilities offered through the Internet and other technologies have become a challenge for traditional higher education institutions, yet providing brand new opportunities for learners. In the case of Turkey, the Human Development Report 2004 for information and communication technologies (ICT) indicated that "with a cautionary, caring, informed and well-rounded approach, communication and Information Technologies can make substantial contributions to Turkey's human development" (UNDP, 2004, p. v). However, the report also warned that:

> Turkey's approach to policy surrounding the use of ICT within education should not therefore be driven by a need to keep pace with international developments but should be led by the need to find appropriate niches where ICT can enhance Turkey's multiple yet specific educational needs. (pp. 48–49)

The mid-2000s in Turkey witnessed many traditional universities' primary efforts to integrate online education modules in response to the needs of geographically dispersed students with a differing profile from traditional students, embracing a multi-dimensional interaction opportunity between and among learners, instructors

S. Yildirim (✉)
Middle East Technical University, Ankara, Turkey
e-mail: soner@metu.edu.tr

M. Adnan
Muğla Sıtkı Koçman University, Ankara, Turkey
e-mail: muge@mu.edu.tr

© The Author(s) 2019
O. Zawacki-Richter and A. Qayyum (eds.), *Open and Distance Education in Asia, Africa and the Middle East*, SpringerBriefs in Open and Distance Education,
https://doi.org/10.1007/978-981-13-5787-9_13

and media, offering flexibility, individualisation, and cost-effectiveness. Yet, as Kondakci, Bedenlier, and Aydin indicated in their contribution to this volume, the 'distance education' adventure for Turkey dates back to the 1920s. After the proclamation of the Turkish Republic in 1923, a well-organised and effective education was of paramount importance for the young national, secular, and democratic state. The government's efforts to restructure the higher education system were grounded on Professor Albert Malche's report on Turkish university reform, and with the valuable contribution of John Dewey, 'distance education' was prioritised among other alternatives to reach all segments of society in the shortest time, particularly for teacher-training activities towards the aim for national literacy. Yet, low literacy rates made it impossible to consider correspondence education until the 1950s (Adnan, 2016).

The initial years of distance education in Turkey were challenging due to the limited available resources of the period. Yet, increasing demand for higher education required additional measures to increase capacity, and facilitate higher education accessibility to the larger audience. Hence, as pointed out by Kondakci, Bedenlier, and Aydin, universities were bestowed the legal responsibility for distance higher education in 1981, and Internet-based distance education has become increasingly important and communal as a natural consequence of the development of accessible information and communication technologies since the mid-90s. Soon enough, the Internet became an integral part of daily life at most Turkish universities. Besides fully online distance education programmes offered at the associate, undergraduate and graduate levels by Turkish higher education institutions, many universities have also integrated online technologies into on-campus teaching for delivering certain courses fully online or in blended learning environments.

Major affordances of distance education such as time and space flexibility, and particularly effective solutions for logistics and instructor shortages have led higher education institutions to transform compulsory common courses at the undergraduate level into fully online courses delivered synchronously or merely asynchronously. Such adoption of online learning technologies requires meticulous strategic planning covering the establishment of a sound technological infrastructure, orientation of instructors and students, the professional development of instructors in order to teach online competently, and most importantly the adequate design and development of content and instructional materials. Several universities have acknowledged their institutional, technological or manpower shortcomings, and formed official collaboration with other universities to utilise their established technological infrastructure or their human resources for online teaching. Nevertheless, this has not always been the case, with many institutions starting out with inadequately designed courses, untrained online instructors and unprepared online learners, which resulted in poor and unsatisfactory teaching-learning experiences through mere online replication of conventional classroom environments (Adnan, 2018; Bates & Sangrà, 2011). This has also resulted in a resistance to online teaching and learning both by instructors and learners.

Online distance education remains as a significant alternative for the Turkish Education System. With more than 17 million students and teachers in K-12 schools, and nearly 6 million students in higher education, the Turkish education system remains a big one. In order for this mass population to access quality education, online distance education may become a great opportunity for those who are especially in the disadvantaged group to access to formal education. On the other hand, the successful integration of Internet-based distance learning programmes, as with any innovative initiatives on this scale, is dependent upon thorough planning, a sound technological infrastructure, high-quality content, and most importantly, acceptance, readiness, and active involvement of administrators, instructors, and learners. If Turkey wishes to reach the greater masses, providing them with effective learning opportunities and not merely ticking the boxes for the required numbers, the next step in Turkey's Internet-based distance education journey needs to focus carefully on quality assurance, considering all factors that impact on both educational settings and products at all stages of e-learning.

References

Adnan, M. (2016). *E-Learning at higher education: A roadmap for Turkish higher education institutions*. Istanbul: Kriter Yayınları.

Adnan, M. (2018). Professional development in the transition to online teaching: Voice of entrant online instructors. *ReCALL, 30*(1), 88–111.

Bates, A., & Sangrà, A. (2011). *Managing technology in higher education: Strategies for transforming teaching and learning*. San Francisco: Jossey-Bass/John Wiley & Co.

Langenberg, D. N., & Spicer, D. Z. (2001). The modern campus. *New Directions for Higher Education, 115*, 3–15.

UNDP. (2004). *Information and communication technologies: Human development report turkey 2004*. Retrieved from http://planipolis.iiep.unesco.org/upload/Turkey/Turkey%20HDR%202004.pdf.

Chapter 14
The State of Open and Distance Education

Adnan Qayyum and Olaf Zawacki-Richter

This book is the second of two volumes. However, these books do not represent an exhaustive portrait of the state of open and distance education (ODE) in the world. Important ODE developments in Indonesia, France, Spain, Mexico, Argentina, Nigeria, Tanzania and many other countries are not covered. However, Australia, Brazil, Canada, China, Germany, India, Russia, South Africa, South Korea, Turkey, United Kingdom, and the United States represent 51% of the world's population. As such, the two volumes about these 12 countries provide a portrait of open and distance education in a large part of the world today. The books also provide an opportunity to compare the trends, challenges and opportunities in ODE based on common points of reference (Raivola, 1985). In this chapter, we compare and analyze ODE enrollments, the relationship of ODE to higher education systems, the growing competition within ODE, the acceptance of ODE, the use of ICTs, and important barriers, challenges and opportunities in these twelve countries.

Growing Enrollments

The overall trend is one of continued growth in ODE enrollments for higher education students. Based on the data provided by the authors, there are over 23 million higher education students taking a distance education course from institutions in the twelve countries (see Table 14.1). This is likely low calculation of total enrollments. It has been hard to tally the precise number of students enrolled in ODE, as countries count

A. Qayyum (✉)
Penn State University, State College, PA, United States
e-mail: adnan@psu.edu

O. Zawacki-Richter
Carl Von Ossietzky University of Oldenburg, Oldenburg, Germany
e-mail: olaf.zawacki.richter@uni-oldenburg.de

© The Author(s) 2019
O. Zawacki-Richter and A. Qayyum (eds.), *Open and Distance Education in Asia, Africa and the Middle East*, SpringerBriefs in Open and Distance Education, https://doi.org/10.1007/978-981-13-5787-9_14

Table 14.1 Enrollment in open and distance education

Country	Enrollment in ODE
Australia	261,000
Brazil	1,341,800
Canada	361,000
China	6,450,000
Germany	154,300
India[a]	4,200,000
Russia	2,475,500
South Africa	337,900
South Korea	298,600
Turkey	1,374,300
United Kingdom	173,900
United States	5,828,800
Total	23,257,100

[a]For India as for other countries, there are different enrollment numbers provided. The ones included here are a more conservative calculation provided by the Government of India's post hoc five-year plan analysis

ODE differently. In Turkey, for example, there is precise data for open education enrollments. Open education is mainly self-paced learning using educational media. But open education is a specified, if dominant, form of DE in the country. However, there is also DE in Turkey that is delivered via synchronous ICTs. In Australia and the UK, the data does not consistently include ODE enrollments on conventional campus-based institutions.

The year over year enrollments in distance education have been growing in most countries. Enrollment has been growing most rapidly in emerging economies. In Brazil, China, and Turkey, ODE enrollments have been increasing dramatically. In Brazil, ODE enrollments grew at 63.8% per year from 2003 to 2009, before tempering to average annual growth rate of 9.9% from 2009 to 2014. In China, ODE enrollments have grown by an average of 8.8% per year from 2004 to 2016. In Turkey, open education enrollments have grown by 20.1% from 2008 to 2014. In these countries, ODE growth is important to meet the increased demand for education that is occurring in tertiary education, and likely all levels of education.

There has been steady growth in ODE enrollments in Australia, Canada, Germany, India and United States for many years. Demand for ODE is growing because of conventional higher education students seeking more flexibility, and adult learners regularly returning to higher education. In South Africa and South Korea enrollment levels have been fluctuating. In South Africa, enrollments at the University of South Africa, by far the biggest DE provider, have been mainly increasing for most of this decade, with the exception of 2014. In South Korea, enrollment numbers have been steady but flat for the past six years from the 17 cyber-universities, while enrollment has been declining at the Korean National Open University.

ODE enrollment numbers have been declining for several years in Russia and the United Kingdom, but for different reasons. Earlier in this book, Zawacki-Richter et al., state that in Russia, ODE enrollments have bifurcated. Demand for online education is growing while demand for correspondence education is declining. Online education includes e-learning, blended learning and flexible learning. It is called *distantsionnoe obrazovanie* to distinguish modern ODE from correspondence education. The latter still connotes the Soviet system of DE and sometimes has a negative image. Educational institutions are growing their offerings *distantsionnoe obrazovanie* and moving away from correspondence education. Despite the growth in *distantsionnoe obrazovanie*, the overall enrollments in all DE formats have been declining in Russia. The substantial ongoing decrease in the country's population has resulted in less demand for education at all levels. Correspondence education seems to be particularly affected by this population decline. In the United Kingdom, a decrease in distance education enrollments is likely attributable to government economic austerity policies in 2011 and 2012 that resulted in increased fees for students since 2012. Gaskell points out, in volume 1, that since those policies, fewer adult students and part-time students, important ODE constituents, have been enrolling. Across the world, there may be other cases like Russia and the UK. But overall, the trend seems to be more ODE enrollment growth than decline.

ODE Growth as Part of Education Growth at All Levels

Education as a sector has seen increased demand for decades (see Fig. 14.1). In primary, secondary and tertiary (or higher) education the number of people enrolled has continued to increase for 50 years. This is due to several factors including: global population growth (in 1965 the global population was 3.3 billion and by 2014 was 7.2 billion people); international efforts encouraging educational participation, like the Millennium Development Goals in 2000 and Sustainable Development Goals from 2015; government educational policies; and a growing general belief that education is important for the (knowledge) economy. However, tertiary education has been growing especially quickly in the past twenty years.

In 1995, only 12.5% of students who finished primary education persisted to higher education (see Table 14.2). Two decades later nearly 30% of people who enroll in primary education enroll in higher education. It is not just that education enrollments are growing but students in education are persisting to higher levels of education.

This has led to increased demand for higher education in countries. In 1992, five countries had more than 50% of their student-aged population attending university. By 2012, 54 countries had more than 50% of their student-aged population attending university (The Economist, 2015). This does not include the demand for higher education by adult learners. This global growth in tertiary education has put pressure

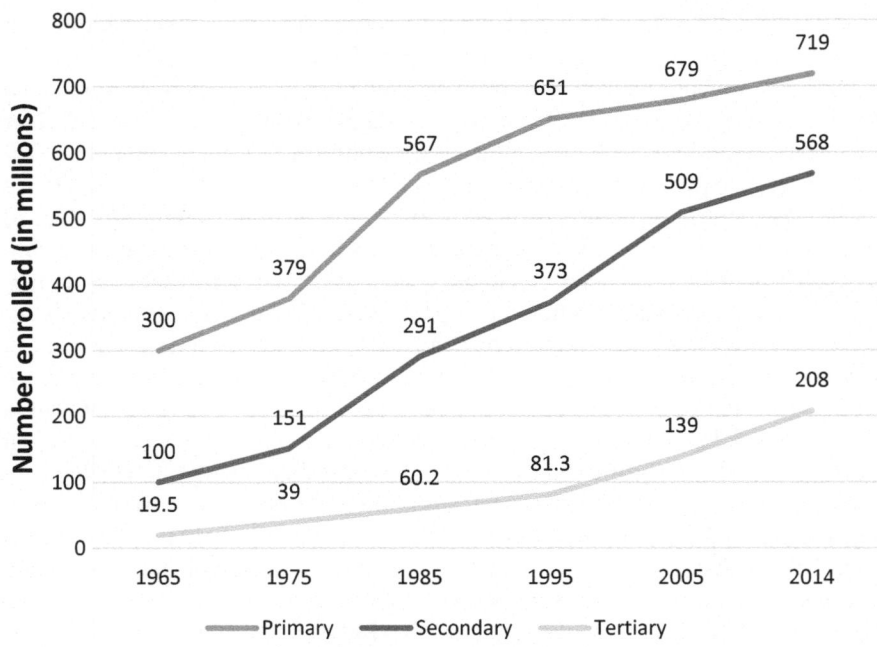

Fig. 14.1 Global gross education enrollment

Table 14.2 Gross education enrollment growth 1965–2014

Year	Primary (millions)	Secondary (millions)	Tertiary (millions)	Primary persisting to secondary (%)	Secondary persisting to tertiary (%)	Primary persisting to tertiary (%)
1965	299.9	100.5	19.5	33.3	19.5	6.5
1975	379.4	151.3	39.0	39.8	25.8	10.3
1985	567.6	291.1	60.2	51.3	20.7	10.6
1995	650.9	373.2	81.3	57.3	21.8	12.5
2005	678.9	509.1	139.3	75.0	27.3	20.5
2014	719.1	568.0	207.5	79.0	36.6	28.9

Source Figures from, and calculations based on, *UNESCO Statistical Yearbook 1979, 1998, 2016*

on educational providers to keep pace with demand as more of the world wants to go to university. DE is seen as a way to meet demand for higher education more quickly while requiring less physical infrastructure and less cost. DE is growing perhaps as an alternative to face-to-face education, but also because education as a whole is growing. DE may have a bigger share of the education pie, but the pie itself is getting bigger.

Globally, enrollments in higher education have been growing faster than any other level of education. From 1995 to 2014, enrollments have grown in primary education by 9.5%, in secondary education by 34.3% and in higher education by 60.9% (UNESCO, 2016). This is partly because of the success of primary and secondary education. For the past two decades, there has been a global push to have more students enter and complete education (e.g. Universal Primary Education initiative, the second goal in the United Nations Millennium Development Goal from the year 2000). This has led to an upward push in persistence, completion and demand in education. As more people complete primary education, the demand for secondary education and later tertiary education has increased. Combined with the growing economic and social importance of higher education credentials, demand is so robust, many countries cannot build conventional tertiary education spaces quickly enough to keep apace. In countries like China and India, distance education offerings are expanding to meet this growing demand.

ODE as Part of Higher Education

It is not just the enrollment figures that matter. In several countries, ODE enrollments are a sizable portion of higher education. Figure 14.2 indicates the percentage of higher education students enrolled in open, online and distance education courses. The percentage ranges from 5.5% of higher education students in Germany taking ODE courses to nearly 50% of all higher education students in Russia taking ODE courses. An average of 21.3% of higher education students were taking ODE courses among the 12 countries.

On the demand side, these figures suggest that open and distance education is increasingly a part of higher education in most countries. In Australia, Brazil, Canada, China, India, Russia, South Africa, Turkey and the United States nearly one fifth or more of all higher education students are taking some online or distance education courses and programs. In the United States, the only growth in higher education enrollments is due to growth in distance education enrollments. On the supply side, distance education is not only being offered by open access, or low-selectivity institutions. In Australia, Brazil, Canada, China, Russia, South Korea the United Kingdom and the United States, high profile institutions are offering distance education. They are providing distance education not only for adult learners, but for younger conventional higher education students wanting flexibility. Both from a student and institutional perspective, distance education is increasingly seen as part of higher education.

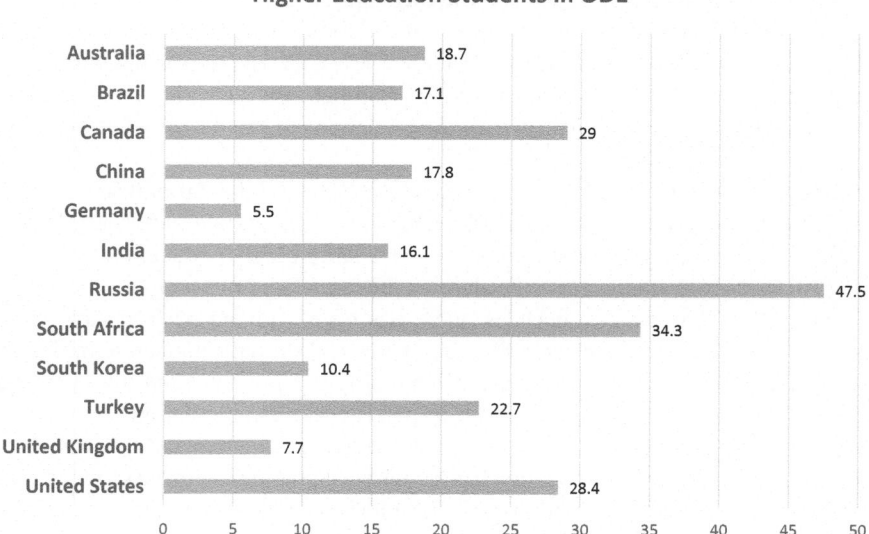

Fig. 14.2 Percentage of higher education students taking open, online or distance education courses

The Ascendance of Online Education

The book chapters reveal that there is a substantial movement towards online education by ODE providers. This is not universal. Distance education is not the same as online education. Forms of DE, other than online education, are still important. One can draw a spectrum of the type of ICTs used to deliver ODE based on the descriptions provide for each country in the books.

As Fig. 14.3 indicates, several countries like South Korea, Australia, Canada and the United States have moved heavily into online education, almost to the exclusion of correspondence education. Other countries like India, China and South Africa are still strongly committed to correspondence education and the use of broadcast radio and television for distance education. Some DE providers continue to be committed to correspondence education not because they are opposed to online education or because they are risk-averse. First, it is not feasible to move towards online, mobile or other digital-based distance education delivery. Uneven access and use of the internet persist, despite increased connectivity in most countries. As indicated in Fig. 14.4, the internet is used regularly by nearly 80% of people in Europe and by over 20% of people in Africa.[1]

---

[1]For details about definitions of internet use, developed and developing countries and methodologies for determining use see: http://www.un.org/esa/sustdev/natlinfo/indicators/methodology_sheets/econ_development/internet_users.pdf.

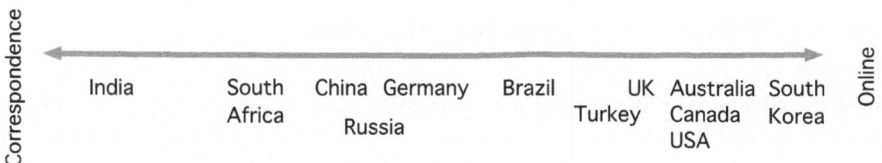

Fig. 14.3 Spectrum of ICT use for open and distance education, by country

On aggregate, nearly 84% of people in developed countries were using the internet and 41% of people in developing countries were. Access to the internet varies in important ways that make it a poor choice, and at times prohibitive, for distance education provision in many countries.

Second, many ODE institutions have long running infrastructure that supports correspondence and broadcast education. The challenge is how to decide what formats to use for course production and delivery when there are so much sunk costs for existing formats. For example, the University of South Africa, the largest DE provider in South Africa, has huge buildings for printing course materials. Any financial calculation about future programs needs to include these legacy infrastructures that may make it more financially beneficial to continue with correspondence education. But sunk costs are also an issue for online education. There is a prohibitive cost of transferring to, for example, a new learning management system.

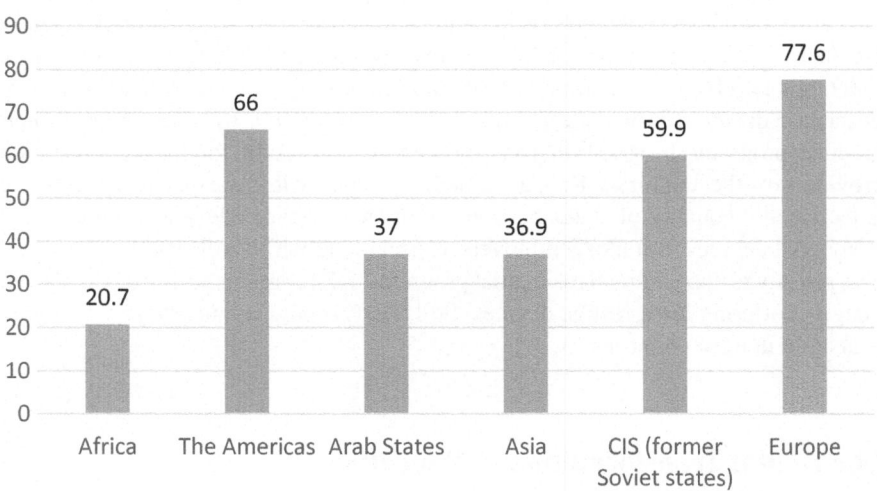

Fig. 14.4 Percentage of people using the internet. *Source* International Telecommunications Union *Facts and Figures* (2016)

The Mainstreaming of Distance Education

With the advent of online education in particular, distance education programs have more legitimacy from larger educational institutions, governments and employers. In countries like Canada, the United States and the United Kingdom, a degree or diploma or other credential does not indicate if it was done via distance education. This has been the case for decades in some institutions. Increasingly, employers and other educators recognize the parity of ODE, or at least do not diminish the legitimacy of learning via distance education. There is no important economic opportunity difference between getting a degree or diploma via ODE or on campus. The output is the same. But the flexibility, time savings, and sometimes, costs savings, make ODE the preferred option for many students. Indeed, in the United States, distance education is seen to be adequately important that the National Center for Education Statistics Integrated Postsecondary Education System is now collecting data about it. This is not the case in all countries. In the United Kingdom and Australia, there is increasing awareness that not tracking online enrollments and providers is a gap in data. In most developed countries, distance education has become an important part of higher education. DE has gained mainstream acceptance.

This is not universally the case. In India, it is still a struggle to get distance education programs and degrees recognized as being of equal value as on-campus programs and degrees. In India, this is expressed by Panda and Garg, in their chapter, as concerns about "parity of esteem". The esteem accorded distance education is not on par with that of residential degrees. This view comes from government bodies like the University Grants Commission, the Indian higher education regulator, that deems DE lacks quality programs for both correspondence and online education. Since 2009, this regulator has banned M.Phil. and Ph.D. programs via distance learning. Distance education providers in India have not been able to offer or grow their graduate programs, programs that have proved very successful for distance education providers in other countries. Kondakci, Bedenlier and Aydin state that in Turkey, there is technically equality of status between open and distance education degrees, and residential degrees. But most employers, especially in white-collar professions, still give priority to conventional residential programs. DE programs still struggle with an image of offering low-prestige degrees. Still, ODE is now an integral part of higher education in most countries.

The Digital Transformation of Education

The growth of ODE enrollments, increased number of ODE providers, and growing acceptance of ODE in most countries is part of a larger digital transformation of education. Certainly, in many countries, ODE growth is partly attributable to increased persistence of students from primary and secondary onto tertiary education. However, in most countries, the growth of ODE is strongly connected to the growth of online education. And online education is part of digital transformation of higher education.

To varying degrees, all countries are encountering social and economic change due to digitization. In education, digitization has become a part of most educational functions, especially in higher education (Altbach, Reisberg, & Rumbley, 2009). Selwyn (2014) argues that most functions in tertiary educational institutions are deeply digitized, including research (i.e. gathering, storing and analyzing research data, writing and publishing reports and articles), administration (i.e. promotion and marketing, registering, enrolling and managing students, etc.), libraries (i.e. online journals and books) and, of course, communication among students, instructors, administrators and researchers. Countries differ in how much education in general and ODE in particularly have been changed by digitization. In some countries, the digital transformation of higher education is well under way while other countries are still early in their use of ICTs and its impact on higher education. The digital transformation of education is strongest in South Korea, the United States, Canada, Australia and the United Kingdom. Countries like India and South Africa are moving in this direction at a slower pace, but definitely have increased digitization of educational processes. In China and Russia, there are concerted efforts by governments and higher education institutions to digitize more educational functions, including teaching. In all countries studied, the teaching function is not immune to the digitization of education. Teaching is increasingly digitized both for on-campus and off-campus students. The growth of distance education is another instantiation of digital processes and practices in education, manifest in the growth of online education. The growth and acceptance of distance education seems to be a symptom of this digital transformation of all education.

Growing Competition in ODE

Competition for providing ODE has been growing. In most countries in the world, an increasing number of institutions are providing online and distance education. Provision of open and distance education courses and programs are available from three major types of institutions: existing institutions, new dual-mode institutions, and new institutions.

Institutions that have historically offered ODE are still important providers. In most cases, they have been growing the number of programs and courses being offered. In the Australia chapter in volume one for example, Latchem stated that almost 75% of all online enrollments are from six universities: Central Queensland University, Charles Sturt University, Deakin University in Melbourne, University of New England, University of Southern Queensland, and the University of Tasmania. In Turkey and South Africa, Anadalou University and UNISA, respectively, are by far the largest providers of distance education. In India, open universities like the Indira Gandhi National Open University (IGNOU) and Yeshvantrao Chavan Maharashtra Open University each have more than half a million students, while four other open universities continue to be growing providers with well over 100,000 students each (CEMCA, 2016).

However, more campus-based institutions are offering ODE, mainly as online education. Over 80% of higher education institutions in Europe offer online courses to distance students (Gaebel, Kupriyanova, Morais, & Colucci, 2014, p. 7). The numbers are similar in the United States. Of the institutions with more than 1000 students, more than 80% of them offer distance education courses (Seaman, Allen, & Seaman, 2018). In Canada and the United States, on-campus institutions are the largest providers of distance education, in the form of online education. As Li and Chen state earlier in this book, in China, high profile campus-based institutions like Peking University, Nanjing University, Sun Yat-Sen University, Beijing Normal University and the Harbin Institute of Technology all offer online education programs. Similarly, in South Africa, the University of Cape Town, which regularly ranks first among universities in all of the African continent, has moved into offering online distance education since 2014. For decades in Russia, most higher education institutions have had distance education units, next to their "direct departments", historically offering correspondence courses. These universities are now some of the main providers of online education. In India, while there are 15 open universities, there are more than 100 dual mode universities, that offer on campus and distance education. Distance education is firmly ensconced in an increasing number of conventional higher educational institutions. Indeed, the term "dual-mode" institutions may now be unnecessary.

There are two major types of new institutions offering online and distance education: institutions created by universities, and institutions created by companies. The emergence of online spin-off institutions, from existing higher education providers, is likely most well known in the MOOC world, with Stanford University spin-offs Coursera and Udacity, and EdX as an MIT initiative. However, it is not a recent or MOOC idea. This practice has been occurring for decades. Lim, Lee and Choi inform us in the South Korea chapter that cyber-universities were established after 2000 and were accredited by South Korean Ministry of Education, Science and Technology. Cyber-universities are institutions providing online education that are affiliated with a campus-based university. Most are administratively distinct from the campus-based institutions but maintain ties, often being a subsidiary. For example, the Kyung Hee Cyber University is independent but based on the Kyung Hee University in Seoul which has been around since 1949. The Daegu Cyber University was established in 2002 and has close ties with Daegu University, which has been around for over 60 years in Gyeongsang province. The Korea National Open University, the main provider of distance education in the country, has seen enrollments affected by competition from the 17 cyber universities. As Table 14.3 indicates, their enrollments have been increasing most years, while KNOU enrollments have been steadily decreasing for several years.

Private companies are also institutions providing distance education. There are private non-profit and private for-profit educational companies. Private universities usually do not receive public funding from the government. While the University of Phoenix is well known to many western audiences, it is certainly not the largest

Table 14.3 Student population of KNOU and cyber universities

Institutions	2010	2011	2012	2013	2014	2015	2016
Korea National Open University	272,452	268,561	254,652	245,257	227,618	214,347	184,074
Cyber Universities	93,297	103,917	106,080	109,673	109,466	111,924	114,496
Total	365,749	372,478	360,732	354,930	337,084	326,271	298,570

private provider of online and distance education courses. Litto states in volume 1 that private for-profit distance education provision is particularly important in Brazil. In 2002, the Ministry of Education approved 25 institutions that were allowed to offer distance education courses. Of these 25, 16 were public institutions and 9 were private institutions. In 2012, 150 institutions that were allowed to offer DE courses –80 public and 70 private. By 2016, 331 institutions were authorized to offer DE courses, 74 public and 257 private institutions. By 2016, public institutions constituted 22.4% of all institutions offering DE in Brazil and 77.4% were private. This growth in private providers of DE is reflected in the enrollment patterns. In 2009, public providers had 20.6% of online and distance education enrollments. By 2014 they had 10.4% of enrollments. Conversely, private institution enrollments grew from 79.4% of DE students to 89.6% during that same time frame. The net effect is that competition has increased substantially and enrollments in DE offerings from public institutions are decreasing as a percentage of enrollments. Four groups, UNOPAR, Anhanguera, Estácio, and UNIP (Universidade Paulista), have over half of all distance education enrollments in Brazil. Private sector distance education enrollments make up nearly 90% of all DE enrollments, and the four major organizations constitute nearly 60% of the private-sector distance education enrollments in Brazil. Even in Russia, there are more students enrolled in correspondence courses from private institutions than from state universities. Private educational institutions emerge and grow when they are able to meet a demand that public institutions may not be able to.

All of these existing and new providers amount to increased competition in the distance education sector. As enrollments have been growing for distance education in most countries, so has the number of providers. The pie is getting larger and there is more competition for it. However, the nature of the competition also matters. High profile, prestigious, institutions are now offering online education like Beijing Normal University in China, Lomonosov Moscow State University in Russia, the University of Cape Town in South Africa, and some Ivy League institutions in the United States like Columbia University and Harvard's extension school. Existing distance education providers now have to consider "brand" and institutional trust as a part of the competitive landscape.

Meeting the Challenges for ODE

Past and current trends in ODE in the 12 countries analyzed indicate that enrollment growth and digital changes in ODE will likely continue. Globally the appetite of ODE is robust, as the demand and acceptance for distance education grows in most countries. While the future of ODE seems strong, not all current providers of ODE may have a future. The current changes are not inevitable and there are many important issues for countries and institutions to address, including competition, strategic responses, and regulations.

The competition for ODE offerings is from current providers, new entrants, and also possible substitutes from current offerings. In most countries, current providers of ODE are visible or at least readily identifiable. Orr, Weller and Farrow (2017) identify three important dimensions of provision in online, open and flexible higher education by current providers: the delivery of learning, content development, and recognition of learning. Most existing ODE organizations are making ongoing changes to their delivery formats in response to changes in demand, and the digital transformation of education. There are many examples of this in all of the 12 countries analyzed. In Australia, for example, Latchem points out that the boundaries between conventional higher education and distance education are blurring. This is in response to a common theme from all countries studied: the strong demand by students for more flexibility because most students, not just conventional ODE students, want more convenient and accessible offerings. This is increasingly achieved by offering more blended formats of educational programs using digital technologies. This will likely continue to be an expansion area from current providers of ODE.

Many educators seem to be fond of thinking of online education as having the potential to be a "disruptive innovation", based on Harvard University business professor Clayton Christensen's work (2011). A disruptive innovation is an innovation that disrupts and overtakes existing organizations and products. Indeed, Christensen himself has written about online education, and been involved with online education initiatives, in this vein. But current educational institutions providing ODE, need to ask if they are the disruptors or the disrupted. In each country, there are new entrants to ODE, both from within countries and, in some cases, international initiatives. In many cases these new entrants are private for-profit educators or partnerships between conventional educational organizations and private companies. As Li and Chen state, Peking University has partnered with Alibaba Group, the largest e-commerce retailer in the world to create Chinese MOOCs. FutureLearn is a for-profit division from the UK Open University. They function as an international distance education provider by partnering with "local" universities to deliver existing and new content in countries.

Increased competition is bringing not just more competitors but also more types of distance education offerings. Among the most successful practices by ODE providers is the provision of different types of credentials. While degrees are still the focus of most institutions, many ODE providers are offering an increased number of certificates. These are often specializations in a subject area, but require far less course work for students than a degree. Micro-credentials are also growing. The highest profile online education micro-credentials are the ones offered by MOOCs. These include badges, statements of accomplishments, and verified certificates. They are often competency-based assessments of learning. Credentials other than degrees are promising for many ODE audiences as they require less time and financial commitment. In some countries, such as teacher training certificates for in-service teachers in Brazil, these certificates have educational and economic value for students.

All types of ODE providers, current and new, are subject to government regulations to varying degrees. In Brazil, all distance education courses must be approved by the Ministry of Education. The documents submitted for approval are used to assess: the curriculum, student admission numbers and student selection policy, ongoing student evaluation, attendance control, qualifications of the teaching staff, library and laboratory facilities, and partnerships with other groups. These have to be approved every five years. In China, government regulations are administered by different levels of national and local educational authorities, and include access regulations, price regulations, quality regulations, and information regulations. These barriers can slow the provision of distance education. Or as seen in India, they can stop any provision for graduate programs via distance education.

The major advantage that existing ODE providers have is that they are known and generally trusted. This is extremely important. New providers of online and distance education can be met with resistance, as students want to know that the institution where they got their degree will still be in existence in 10 and 20 years. That trust and familiarity is important but not enough. The digital transformation of education is an opportunity for ODE providers to rethink what their core value proposition is. In all countries, there are more providers of distance education, but there are not necessarily more providers of open education. Distance education has benefited from, and benefited, the digital transformation of education. It is more complicated for open education, an area that has been contested, appropriated and at times marginalized by the digital transformation of education (Weller, 2014).

Overall Changes

Overall, the changes taking place in ODE seem to be driven by four sets of factors, summarized by the acronym VEDI (Latin for "see"):

1. **Values**—the values and vision of educational institutions and policymakers for ODE. There seem to be two major sets of visions among ODE providers: offering open access to potential students who may not otherwise have ready access to education; or providing flexible access to students. Many of the changes taking place for ODE seem to be driven by providing more flexibility for students. But the historical mission and vision of distance education, particularly single-mode institutions, has been about providing openness. These two sets of visions need not be opposed. However, there is certainly concern about the future of openness and single mode ODE universities (Tait, 2018). Open education is still important

for many students served by ODE providers. However, providing flexibility, not openness, seems to be more prioritized by many institutions offering ODE across the globe.

2. Environment—the historical, political and policy environment for open and distance education affects the provision, growth and changes to ODE offerings in all countries. In some countries a highly centralized approach to educational policy regulation continues to define how ODE is allowed to develop. In other places, where education policy regulation is more decentralized, the development and innovation within ODE is emerging at the institutional and local level. Indeed, in many countries, the regulatory environment can seem invisible as local educators and administrators are making key decisions about the development and growth of ODE.

3. Demand—the demand for ODE is emerging from different sources. In some countries, all educational demand is growing and ODE is part of the trend. In other countries, the demand for ODE being driven by demand for flexibility, for lifelong learning, and for different types of certification. ODE growth is benefiting from existing educational demand and partly fostering growing educational demand from lifelong and adult learners.

4. ICTS—the types and level of ICT access that potential students have. In some countries, ICT access is extensively digital, via computers and mobile phones. In these settings, the digital transformation of education has been extensive. Distance education has substantially become online education in these countries, and they are relatively, what Bates (2018) calls, mature markets for online education. In other countries, digital ICT access is growing but not extensive. Online education is still emerging, but other forms of ICTs for ODE continue to be important.

Current Approaches

In this context, educational providers have been both re-active and pro-active in their approach to dealing with increased competition and the changing landscape for ODE. Re-active approaches include, what Orr et al. (2017) have called, "defender-like" competitive strategies. Here, institutions focus on providing ODE to their main constituent of students. They may update and innovate their offerings for, and relationships with, the core student audiences. But the focus is on serving these core audiences that have historically been the priority. Pro-active approaches include what Orr et al. (2017) have called, "prospector-like" competitive strategies. Here, institutions take a more entrepreneurial approach and try to innovate in all areas of their ODE provision. This includes innovating in the delivery and design of offerings (e.g. modules, courses, programs) and certifications. But it also includes new target audiences of students and trying to be revenue generating and profitable.

It can be tempting to advocate that ODE providers need to use only or mainly pro-active approaches in the current ODE landscape. However, the decision to use re-active or pro-active strategies depends not just on the demand for ODE, the policy environment, or the type of ICT access available. It also depends on the values and visions of educators. As the chapters in these volumes indicate, ODE has been changing in a digital age. However, open and distance education has a strong history of being education for those who may not otherwise have an opportunity to education. There is a risk that these values and visions may become secondary priorities or non-priorities, with the strong move globally to online education. Fifty years ago, distance education was transformed by the beginning of the open university movement. This transformation was based on the values and vision of educators. These values and visions need to be just as important as the policy environment, demand, and ICT access, for open and distance education in a digital age.

References

Altbach P. G., Reisberg, L., & Rumbley L. E. (2009). *Trends in global higher educa-tion: Tracking an academic revolution.* Retrieved from http://www.researchgate.net/profile/ Philip_Altbach/publication/225084084_Trends_in_Global_Higher_Education_Tracking_an_ Academic_Revolution/links/551ac4020cf251c35b4f5d0d.pdf.

Bates, T. (2018). The 2017 national survey of online learning in Canadian post-secondary education: methodology and results. *International Journal of Educational Technology in Higher Education* https://doi.org/10.1186/s41239-018-0112-3.

Christensen, C., Horn, M., Caldera, L., & Soares, L. (2011). *Disrupting college: How disruptive innovation can deliver quality and affordability to postsecondary education.* Washington: Center for American Progress.

Commonwealth Educational Media Centre for Asia. (2016). *Status of the State Open Universities in India.* New Delhi: Indira Gandhi National Open University.

The Economist. (2015). *The World is Going to University.* March 26.

Gaebel, M., Kupriyanova, V., Morais, R., & Colucci, E. (2014). *E-learning in European higher education institutions.* Belgium: European University Association.

International Telecommunication Union. (2016). *Measuring the information society report 2016.* https://www.itu.int/en/ITU-D/Statistics/Documents/.../misr2016/MISR2016-w4.pdf.

Orr, D., Weller, M., & Farrow, R. (2017). *Models for online, open, flexible and technology enhanced higher education—Results of a global analysis.* Presentation at the World Conference on Online Learning. Toronto: Canada.

Porter, M. (1998). *Competitive strategy: Techniques for analyzing industries and competitors.* New York: The Free Press.

Raivola, R. (1985). What is comparison? Methodological and philosophical considerations. *Comparative Education Review, 29*(3), 362–374.

Seaman, J. E., Allen, I. E., & Seaman, J. (2018). *Grade increase: Tracking distance education in the United States.* Wellesley: The Babson Survey Research Group.

Selwyn, N. (2014). *Digital technology and the contemporary university: Degrees of digitization.* London: Routledge.

Tait, A. (2018). Open Universities: The next phase. *Asian Association of Open Universities Journal, 13*(1) https://doi.org/10.1108/AAOUJ-12-2017-0040.

UNESCO. (2016). *Statistical yearbook* (2016th ed.). New York: United Nations.
Weller, M. (2014). *The battle for open: How openness won and why it doesn't feel like victory.* London: Ubiquity Press.